MANAGEMENT CONSULTANCY

For my parents-in-law
Adam and Ann Czerniawski

Management Consultancy

What Next?

Fiona Czerniawska

palgrave

First published 2002 by
PALGRAVE
Houndmills, Basingstoke, Hampshire RG21 6XS and
175 Fifth Avenue, New York, N. Y. 10010
Companies and representatives throughout the world

PALGRAVE is the new global academic imprint of St. Martin's Press LLC Scholarly and Reference Division and Palgrave Publishers Ltd (formerly Macmillan Press Ltd).

ISBN 0–333–97112–4

This book is printed on paper suitable for recycling and made from fully managed and sustained forest sources.

A catalogue record for this book is available from the British Library.

Library of Congress Cataloging-in-Publication Data
A catalogue record for this book is available from the Library of Congress

Formatted by
The Ascenders Partnership, Basingstoke

10 9 8 7 6 5 4 3 2 1
11 10 09 08 07 06 05 04 03 02

Printed and bound in Great Britain by
Creative Print and Design (Wales),
Ebbw Vale

Contents

Preface

If there's one mistake *Management Consultancy in the 21st Century* made, it was to underestimate the impact that e-business would have on the consulting industry. Although many of the strategic issues identified in the book remain as true in 2001 as they were in 1999, it is e-business that has been the main driver for change, creating opportunities for new entrants to establish themselves faster in the consulting industry than would have been dreamed possible even a decade ago, and challenging established firms to develop new services and find new means to deliver them. E-business is, I shall argue, raising fundamental questions about the nature of consultancy.

Nor are these questions becoming any less valid as the dot.com boom rapidly turns to bust.

E-business has changed irreversibly, if not the underlying economic laws that govern us as a whole, then – at the very least – the bounds of what individual organisations believe is possible. In the late 1990s, the press abounded with stories about the difficulty large corporations were having in finding the 'e-people' required by the new economy, people who were highly flexible, who were prepared to bear responsibility and risk, who were prepared to act on faith rather than hard data. 'Old economy' people, accustomed to being bolstered by chains of command and procedures designed to manage risk, were – we were told – transparently unsuited to this new regime. Yet the practical experience since 1999 has been very different: far from being reluctant to enter the fray, most organisations have found that their staff have been only too happy to work differently. 'It's been like freeing the slaves in nineteenth century America', said one person I talked to. 'Once something like that's happened, you can't put the clock back'.

The problem with e-business was that we talked in terms of absolutes, when in fact the changes were relative ones. 'Internet time' is a good example: three months from inception to launch became the benchmark by which e-business ventures were judged. Wait any longer and the world will have moved on, was the message. But now it appears that the importance of Internet time lay in the extent to which it forced established corporations to do something in time scales which, a couple of years earlier, would have been regarded as hopelessly unrealistic. It's been this relative change of pace – not the absolute pace of change – that has long-lasting significance in the economy. E-business has changed the rules – just not the rules we thought it had changed.

The same is true in the consulting industry. In 1998, when *Management Consultancy in the 21st Century* was written, e-business was a minority interest: only a couple of those interviewed then saw the Internet as having any significance for the consulting industry. Yet the three years since those interviews took place have been a period of considerable change within the consulting industry. Initially, the new entrants caught the market by surprise, specialising in fields that many of their older, more generalist rivals were struggling to service; more recently, the tables appear to have turned as clients increasingly recognise that, if the 'new' economy is to yield any sustainable benefits, it will only do so in conjunction with 'old' economy disciplines. Many of the new firms have already seen their stock prices tumble: some will not survive. But the impact of e-business will outlast its individual evangelists. As with the economy as a whole, you can't put the clock back.

The aim of this substantially revised edition of *Management Consultancy in the 21st Century* is to ask: what next? What are the key issues for the consulting profession as it passes the first to the second generation of e-business?

As with the first edition, the intention here is to present a plurality of views. Thus, this book begins with a survey of the impact of e-business and analyses the latter's impact on the strategic issues identified in the first edition. However, the second part of the book is given over to a new set of interviews, again with leading consultants – managers, practitioners and commentators – from around the world. As before, these people speak for themselves.

Acknowledgements

Enormous thanks go to those people who were prepared to give up their time to speculate about the future and whose comments make up the second half of this book. But I'd also like to express my appreciation to all the other people who helped make those interviews happen and in particular: Kate Cleevely at the Weber

Group, Wendy Miller and Christina Wallace at Bain & Company, Warren Lewis at Cap Gemini Ernst & Young, Joan Lufrano at DiamondCluster, Ellen Ringel at Deloitte Consulting, Lex Melzer at KPMG, Andrew Giangola at McKinsey & Company, Corrinne Milsom-Mann at Mercer Management Consulting, and Jennifer Abbott at Manning Selvage & Lee.

I'd also like to thank Stephen Rutt and his colleagues at Palgrave for all their commitment and support, and my husband, Stefan, for all of his.

1

Introduction: Where Are We Now?

The Big 'E': 1999 – March 2000

'E-business changed everything', said one senior consultant I talked to. 'We had to refocus everything we did. It challenged who we were and what value we could bring to clients.'

The late 1990s saw the emergence of a whole new generation of consulting firms – firms like IXL, Sapient, Scient and Razorfish – all of whom were growing phenomenally fast, even by the generous standards of the conventional consulting industry. They were walking through a door thrown open by clients dissatisfied with the level of e-business expertise on offer from the majority of their existing advisers. What these clients wanted was in-depth, specialist knowledge of e-business and hands-on, practical experience of implementing e-business ideas. What they didn't want – and this is what they largely saw themselves getting – were ERP consultants, who'd received token e-business retraining and whose services were little more than a firm's existing portfolio, with an 'e' stuck on the front. 'Pigs with lipstick' is how one person put it in retrospect. By contrast, these new firms appeared to offer fresh ideas, a new way of doing things and, above all, a dedicated focus on the new economy.

The impact of such firms has been considerable, whatever the level of their stock price in 2001, but it lies less in their speed of growth or in the inroads they were able to make into the consulting market. Instead, I'd argue their significance lies in the extent to which they self-consciously set out to redefine the meaning of consulting. Remember Andersen Consulting's (now Accenture) advertisements in the early 1990s? 'Metamorphosis in a world of change.' The meaning was far less important than the message they sent out to the firm's clients, competitors and employees: that this was a firm that was capable of and willing to take the high ground. The same was true of the e-specialist firms that emerged at the end of the 1990s: much of their significance lay in the fact that they were willing to talk about the consulting industry and their role in it. In an industry which had historically prided itself on working invisibly, behind the scenes, facilitating the success of clients rather than broadcasting their own, it was talking like this, rather than the content of what was said, that was genuinely revolutionary.

The e-specialist firms changed the rules and raised the stakes. Their position demanded a response, and they got one. By mid-1999, established firms were starting – slowly but relentlessly – to change course.

They were led by the strategy firms: not surprisingly, as strategy was the area in which e-business first made its presence felt and, by early 2000, the level of e-business work undertaken by such firms was typically between 35 and 40 per cent. It was a market that most firms believed played firmly to their various strengths. 'E-business', said Chris Zook, the head of Bain & Co's e-commerce practice in the spring of 2000, 'is a huge factor in the consciousness of the firm.'[1] As he saw it, the demands of e-business clients matched perfectly with Bain's entrepreneurial culture: 'we're accustomed to taking risk and delivering results. And the world is going our way: clients are more and more looking for and rewarding entrepreneurialism in consultants. A firm like Bain has never been at its most effective operating in highly bureaucratic organisations.' McKinsey & Co took the same stance, although they saw e-business playing to a different strength. 'Our real strength', commented Ron Farmer, again in early 2000 when he was jointly responsible for @McKinsey, McKinsey's e-business practice, 'lies – as it has always done – in the depth of understanding we have about specific markets … The sheer volatility of the e-business environment makes domain-specific knowledge absolutely essential if a company is to make the right investment decisions. Analysis, judgement and experience are all as important as they used to be – if not more so.'

What changed, then, was not so much the content of what was delivered by strategy consultancies, as the process and manner in which it was delivered. Faced with the apparent imperatives of 'Internet time', many strategy houses found themselves compressing assignments which would have taken several months to complete in the past, into as many weeks. They also had to rethink the nature of their deliverables: detailed strategies were replaced by more dynamic approaches in which the short-term means to the end could shift in line with rapidly changing market conditions.

The technology-based consultancies also enjoyed an immediate benefit from e-business. While lengthy ERP implementations of questionable value and the level of expenditure on Y2K work had severely tarnished the reputation of this sector, e-business helped to repair it. Clients, who were unsure whether web-related technology was simply an enabler for their business or was a genuine driver of change, became willing, once again, to listen to technology experts. Technology itself, which had fallen from most board-level agendas in the 1990s, suddenly became a strategic priority. As a direct result, technology consultants, who had previously found that the level in an organisation at which they had their key relationships was inexorably declining, found themselves talking to the CEO and IT director. And they used this opportunity to sell to clients a far wider range of services (notably strategy, branding and marketing) than would have been the case in the past. Thus, e-business opened up at least a temporary window in which technology-based consultancies could – really for the first time – reposition themselves successfully.

As e-business moved through the consulting value chain, it hit the operationally-based consulting firms next. At roughly the same time that the strategy firms were estimating that between a third and a half of their fee income was e-business related, the operationally-based firms claimed that around a fifth of their work was generated in this way. E-business was perhaps slower to take off for this particular segment of the consulting industry because it bore the brunt of the client dissatisfaction with generalist business or IT consultants who were perceived to have little of specific value to add so far as e-business was concerned. That these firms apparently resembled the large, hierarchically-based corporations of the old economy also counted against them. 'It's not just that we want to buy e-business related services', explained one client at the time. 'We also want to work with consulting firms that offer us a fresh model for doing things – a different culture, a new set of values.'

The incumbents reacted in two ways. Some chose to stick to their knitting, believing that their most effective, long-term positioning would be to reconfigure their existing services for the new market, rather than launch suites of new services. But other firms saw e-business as an opportunity to redefine their role in the wider economy. Such firms were haunted by the explosive growth enjoyed by technology companies during the 1980s and 1990s: while their own business may have grown at around 15 per cent per annum, companies like ERP supplier SAP were growing at many multiples of this at their peak. Never again did they want to miss out on opportunities for growth that dwarfed their own time- and materials-based earning potential. Some consulting firms chose to enter the new economy in their own right.

Sometimes such moves took place in markets adjacent to their core business: Cap Gemini Ernst & Young, for example, launched Netstrike Worldwide, an internet-based company designed to match resource gaps in Fortune 1000 companies with talented individuals who – for a variety of reasons (family, other business commitments, and so on) – had chosen not to enter the full-time workforce. As such, Netstrike provided both a service to CGE&Y's clients and a pool of additional labour that the firm itself could draw on during periods of peak demand. On other occasions, the ventures took the consulting firm well beyond the bounds of which might be traditionally conceived to be consulting. PricewaterhouseCoopers launched E-conomy, offering low-cost office supplies to small and medium-sized enterprises. In doing this, PwC was able to pass on to these companies the bulk discount it was able to negotiate on its own behalf, due to its size. But E-conomy also gave the firm an opportunity to build relationships with companies which, while they had high growth potential, would not be capable of paying for PwC's professional services. In effect, E-conomy has provided PwC with an entry point into a market from which it was largely excluded in the past: it can be no accident that its services were initially aimed at companies in Silicon Valley.

The potential for such ventures was thought to be considerable: CGE&Y, Accenture and PwC were all quoted as saying that they believed that between a fifth and a third of their income would come from non-consulting sources by 2005.

But such strategies weren't simply the seizing of an opportunity. They were also a reaction to the increasing competitiveness of the consulting industry and to the perennial problem – which e-business complicated, rather than resolved – of how consulting firms differentiate themselves.

Consulting firms were essentially competing along one of two axes. The strength of the new e-consultants lay in their in-depth understanding of the new economy: where they were comparatively weak was their brand – something which placed them at a considerable disadvantage, especially where risk-averse clients, facing an uncertain future, were concerned. 'Why should we increase the risk we face,' said one, 'by hiring a firm no one in our organisation has ever heard of, let alone worked with? Our e-business projects are quite high-risk enough, without incurring this extra level of uncertainty.' The imperative for the e-consultancies, therefore, was to increase their familiarity in clients' eyes, to build trust and long-term relationships.

For the incumbent firms, the problem was the reverse: high in terms of brand recognition, many were perceived by clients to be insufficiently specialised. 'We want to work with world-class experts,' explained one client, 'and we just don't believe that a firm which is offering to do everything – one-stop-shopping – will have the depth of expertise we require. They may have some leading thinkers, but they won't have a monopoly of them.' There was a fear of dumbing-down, that such firms did hire experts only to use them on a range of different projects, thus diluting, rather than concentrating, their expertise. Thus, for incumbents, the challenge was internal – to foster specialist skills without losing the operational homogeneity of the firm as a whole. As a result, e-business, rather than leading to greater long-term differentiation in the industry, became a force for convergence, with the majority of firms converging on the same conceptual space (Figure 1.1).

Only the strategy firms seemed immune from the process, already combining high brand recognition with a reputation for being able to field specialists.

Yet, while some facets of e-business consultancy drove firms to become more, not less, alike, others created an opportunity for genuine differentiation. One of the inherent problems about the consulting industry is that it is very hard for any individual firm to resist the

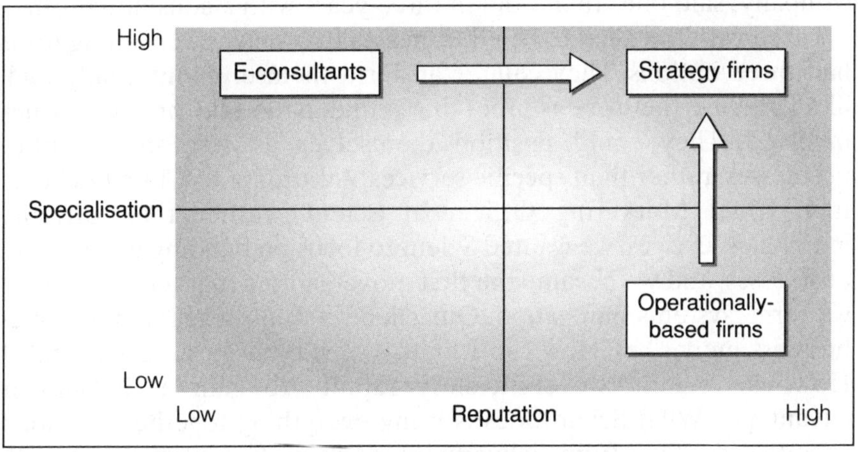

Figure 1.1 *The axes of competition within the consulting industry*

pressure to look like its rivals. Makers of manufactured products have the freedom to produce many product variations precisely because that product is physical, visible, tangible. Thus, a car is still a car, irrespective of its colour, engine power, or high-tech gadgetry. But a consultant who looks very different from other consultants might – in clients' eyes – not be a consultant at all. Make a consulting service unique, and clients might not see it as that service, but something else. It's the invisibility and intangibility of much consultancy that means that, in order to be credible, it has to look the same.

E-business didn't – indeed, couldn't – change this: what it could do is offer a way out. One of the most significant changes in client thinking that e-business has crystallised, if not initiated, is that clients want consulting firms to have put their money where their mouths are, to walk the talk. 'If consultants come to you to sell you a customer relationship management project, then it's legitimate to ask them whether their own firm uses the same package and processes. Why, if they're so confident about the benefits to us, haven't they implemented it for themselves?', was how one client summed it up. It's hard to overstate the significance of this shift: for decades, consultants have been seen as peddlers of theory, going from one company to the next, taking and applying new ideas. But, in the eyes of e-business clients, this was not enough: faced with almost overwhelming uncertainty, they wanted consultants who had actually done something – implemented packages, run e-businesses. It was an attitude reinforced by the plethora of consultants who left the industry to work in dot.coms: 'I've learnt more in three months of running this company', said one, 'than I did in three years with a consulting firm.'

Faced with the need to be e-businesses themselves, consulting firms had three options. They could transform themselves internally, and, like IBM, use the story as proof that it understood the practical issues involved. They could position themselves as creators of entire businesses, rather than specific services. According to Chris Locheed, then Chief Marketing Officer at Scient, 'rather than offering individual services, we wanted Scient to focus on building complete e-businesses, and we became the first movers into a marketspace which we term 'systems innovation'. Our clients ask us: what should my e-business model be? How can I build a new e-business very quickly? How can I innovate sufficiently rapidly to gain a first-mover advantage? What Scient does is bring everything together: we don't decouple strategy from delivery; we don't write a report and walk away. We either build an e-business with a client or we don't work with them: we either engage with the CEO or we walk away. It's the only way we are prepared to work'.

Setting up their own e-businesses has been the third option explored by consulting firms – as ventures like NetStrike and E-Conomy demonstrate: there could be no better proof that a firm was capable of exploiting the potential of the networked economy. Consulting firms cease to be mere spectators on the economic stage and become prime movers in their own right. In *Blown to Bits*, Philip Evans and Thomas Wurster suggest that there are three criteria which will mark out successful companies in the future: their richness (their depth of expertise in their chosen markets); their reach (the breadth and diversity of their customer base); and their affiliation (the extent to which they can overcome the traditional supplier-consumer divide in order to champion their customers' causes). Ironically – given that both Evans and Wurster are consultants with The Boston Consulting Group – it's a model that captures perfectly the opportunity for consulting firms. A good consultant will know as much as, if not more than, his or her client about a specific industry or process ('richness'), but the consultant will have the added advantage of having a far wider range of contacts whom he or she can call on ('reach'). When, last year, I researched a consulting company that had won an industry award for its e-business work, I asked the client what made them so special in their eyes. 'They picked up the phone and corralled their acquaintances on our behalf', said the client. Consultants are far better positioned than their clients to bring together the kind of eclectic eco-systems of companies that will be the prerequisite of success in the networked economy. The only part of the picture so far lacking is 'affiliation' – a reflection of the fact that most consulting firms have chosen to spread their risk by servicing multiple markets simultaneously, rather than ally themselves to any one sector. While becoming more affiliated does expose a firm to changing market conditions, the returns may justify the risk: by seizing the initiative, consulting firms may well turn out to be the holding companies of the future. As such, there's no doubt that this trend has the potential to transform the competitive landscape of the industry.

The Bubble Bursts: April 2000 and Beyond

The pendulum of hype has swung back. At the start of 2000, the column inches dedicated to e-business were seemingly limitless:

unprecedented years of growth suggested that we had entered the 'goldilocks' economy – neither too hot nor too cold, but just right. A year later, the same column inches are full of blow-by-blow accounts of the latest dot.com failure, the latest IPO to be shelved.

And the consulting industry has been caught up in this: the latter half of 2000 saw billions of dollars being wiped from the value of those aggressive, new e-specialists. For most of these firms, retrenchment has become the order of the day. This is taking two forms. First, externally: the level to which the stocks of these firms has dropped is partly connected to the extent to which their business appears to be dependent on dot.coms (who are clearly in no position to buy consultancy). Thus, firms with a greater foothold in the large corporate market have suffered less. Not surprisingly, most of these new entrants are trying to increase their penetration in this sector and have been repositioning their services as a result. Clearly, this threatens to compromise their 'new' economy credentials: how much 'old' economy work can you take on before you cease to be an e-specialist?

The second change is an internal one. Scratch below the surface and it's not hard to find stories from large corporations who have found their dealings with the e-specialists challenging – to say the least. One company I spoke to remembers being hugely impressed by the quality of thinking and innovation brought by one of these companies in the first phase of a project: 'it really was very exciting. They made us question who we are and what we are in business for. The strategic vision they produced was excellent.' What was less excellent was the firm's ability to implement its vision: 'it wasn't so much the technical know-how that was at fault', recalled the client, 'as their lack of process. At one stage, they actually went out and bought some project management books and software. And, when we told them we weren't happy with the situation, they didn't have a process whereby we could escalate the problem internally.' One of the key strengths of the new entrants had been their lack of bureaucracy and the fact that individual consultants were encouraged to take responsibility for their actions, not pass decisions through a long chain of command. But, by the latter part of 2000, this strength was rapidly becoming a weakness in clients' eyes. 'You can get away with not having much in the way of client handling skills or processes in a growing immature market', said another client, 'but these are the kind of things you really need once the environment becomes more complex and difficult.' As a result, many of the new entrants found themselves trying to acquire some of the facets of their more established rivals, by investing in account management processes and by hiring experienced client managers. Again, compromise threatened: how far could you go in replicating the good aspects of your competitors' businesses before you began to mimic their faults?

For the incumbent consulting firms, by contrast, the change offered new possibilities: the world was going their way. While dot.com failures dominated the headlines, large corporations – those behemoths of the 'old' economy – had begun to invest millions of dollars in e-business projects. Many were internal (e-procurement projects offered – and continue to offer – enormous savings); most had a very low public profile; all of them offered opportunities for consultants, especially those firms that could demonstrate that they could bring the best of the new and the old together – innovative thinking implemented with 'old' economy discipline. 'People thought that the new economy heralded the death of process', commented one consultant, a beneficiary of this sea change, 'in fact, e-business projects are so complex and the technology involved is so new, that process matters more than ever.'

The big question now is: what next? E-business has changed the consulting market, but will these changes stick? Are we seeing the beginning of the end of the 'new' economy firms and the resurgence of the established players? Or will at least some of those new firms deliver on what they promised – the redefinition of professional services? Will e-business be the 'big thing' for the consulting industry over the next ten years? Or is there a 'next big thing' out there, waiting to happen?

The aim of this book is to answer these questions in two ways. Like its precursor, it's split into two parts. Part I (What Next?) analyses the short-term future of the consulting industry and looks specifically at the legacy (if that is the correct term) of e-business – its impact on the client-consultant relationship and the strategic challenges it poses for the consulting industry. Part II (And Then What?) is based on interviews with leading management consultants around the world, and takes the process a step further to ask that truly billion dollar question – what comes after e-business?

---

1 Interviewed by the author and originally quoted in *E-Business: Winning Strategies for the New Economy* (Fitzwilliam, NH: Kennedy Information, 2000). The core

Part I

The Changing Structure of Consultancy

2

The Consulting Market: Changes in the Client-Consultant Relationship

The client-consultant relationship is changing fast.

The original edition of this book, *Management Consultancy in the 21st Century*, argued that the 1990–91 recession had begun a trend in which power, in the client-consultant relationship, was shifting from consultants to their clients. But, although an increasing number of books and articles were being published which suggested that client satisfaction was growing, it was argued that, at least in the more mature consulting markets, the underlying relationship between clients and consultants is essentially a symbiotic one. The role of consultants is to fill gaps in the intellectual capital of their clients; but, in filling the gaps of one client, they create gaps in the intellectual capital of others. Thus, when Company A decides it needs to do X, and it hires a consulting firm to help deliver X and Companies B, C and D suddenly become X-less and they too want X, a market is created for the consulting firm to take its X methodology from one client to another. *Management Consultancy in the 21st Century* concluded that, although the process by which X is taken from company to company might speed up (leading to a whole series of potential problems in terms of resources, delivery and quality), the continuous state of 'management uncertainty' meant that there would always be one company with a new problem to solve; and, where one company had a problem, others would soon have it; where one company had a solution, others would soon want it. Consultancy, therefore, is an unstoppable force.

The advent of e-business has gone some way towards proving this hypothesis. Once the economic dust has settled, we may be able to trace the paths by which new ideas in one company (the market innovator) rapidly became sought-after ideas in others (the me-too companies) and the role that consulting firms played in spreading the news.

But e-business also helps to refine this hypothesis further. It has become clear, from interviewing clients as the e-business market evolved, that the nature of the intellectual gaps to be filled has changed considerably since 1998, and that these changes may have significant implications for the client-consultant relationship in the future.

Why Do People Hire Consultants?

Looking at the e-business consulting market, it's possible to identify five distinct categories of intellectual capital 'gaps' – each of which constitutes a reason for bringing in a consultant:

- *Fresh ideas* – some clients genuinely want access to innovative thinking, whether it takes the form of hard data (to help them make a decision, perhaps) or a more creative, facilitative input;
- *Additional resources* – but, particularly in the early stages of an emerging market, what clients are often most short of is people: their own people area is already fully occupied and the company's management may be reluctant to free up too many (with all the disruption it would entail) to pursue largely unproven ideas; in this context, consultancies can supply a useful, generically-qualified pool of short-term labour;
- *Specialist resources* – the fact that clients welcome extra pairs of hands in the early days doesn't blind them to the fact that it is specialist expertise – having access to the know-how they do not have the opportunity to develop by themselves – that makes the difference in the long-run;
- *Structured methodology* – many of those involved in the early stages of e-business thought they could throw away the whole rule book, that e-business changed not just the 'content' of business, but the 'process' by which business was carried out; the collapse of the dot.com market exposed this fallacy, rehabilitated the idea that a structured process was an important contributor to the success of a project, and brought clients back to consulting firms who could demonstrate a tried-and-tested methodology;
- *Contact network* – but the growing influence of method did not completely reverse the effect of e-business; one of the ways in which clients found the input of consultants to be most valuable was in the

creating of the type of cross-sector partnerships underpinning many of the more successful business models to have emerged in the 'new' economy – consultants were simply better connected than the majority of their clients.

The evolution of the e-business market suggests that there are some identifiable trends which have implications for consulting markets in the future. As the e-business market developed, and as clients became more sophisticated purchasers of e-business consultancy (one of the ironies of e-business consulting was that the idea of 'learning at internet speed', propounded by so many consultancies, is that it applied equally to the way in which clients hired consultants), the relative importance of these five reasons changed. In the earliest days, additional resources and new ideas were what clients were looking for most, but, as clients became more aware of the distinctive possibilities of e-business, they looked to consultancies to provide the network of contacts many of their ventures required and the specialist knowledge to help realise them. Innovative thinking became less important because the early adopting clients were moving into implementation mode, and those that followed behind them – the 'me-too' companies – were more interested in copying what the leaders had done, than in developing new ideas of their own. In the later stages, partly as a result of the burgeoning number of dot.com failures, increasingly knowledgeable clients were looking to consultants to provide a structured implementation process – one that increased the chance of success.

Comparing the relative importance of these five factors suggests the following (see also Figure 2.1), that:

- There is an inverse relationship between the desire for additional resources – extra pairs of bright, but unspecifically qualified hands – and the desire for a structured methodology; in other words, clients are willing to use generic labour in an emerging market, when they're trying to feel their way to a solution, but want access to a tried-and-tested methodology as soon as the market shows some signs of maturing;

- A second inverse relationship exists between the desire for innovative thinking and the way in which clients sought to exploit consultants' networks of contacts; although the importance of the network of contacts has been peculiar to e-business, this suggests that in an emerging consulting market, clients begin by looking for new ideas, but then, quite rapidly, move on to extracting something of particular, identifiable value from their consultants.

In both these cases, the maturation of the consulting market is accompanied by a shift in clients' desires, from the general to the specific – from bringing in consultants to help stimulate thinking and provide initial momentum, to hiring them for very specific purposes.

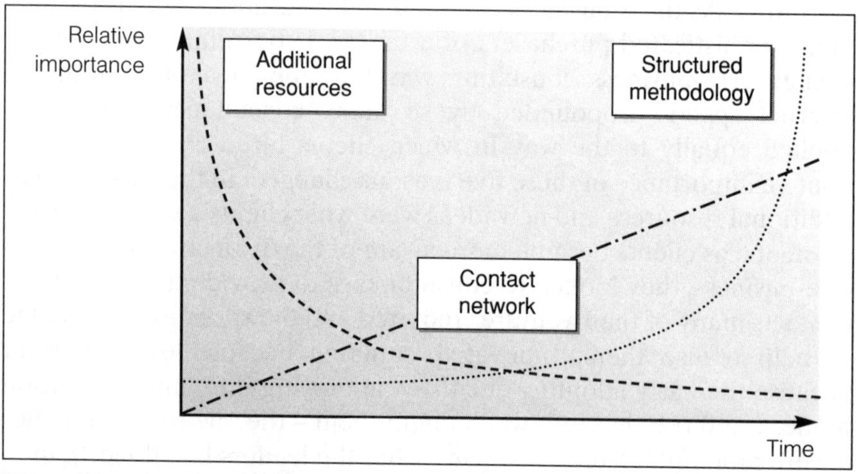

Figure 2.1 *How the relative importance of the reasons for hiring consultants changes as a market matures*

A third inverse relationship is observable when we look at the importance of specialist knowledge.

Clients have always wanted specialist knowledge – often far more than consulting firms have been willing or able to provide. 'What we want', said one client I talked to, 'is to be able to work with the world's leading expert in each field. Specialist knowledge is the most tangible, visible way in which consultants can demonstrate they add value – they tell you something you didn't know, or do something you couldn't do.' As with other trends, e-business has exacerbated, rather than changed, this perception. With so much information available, from so many different sources, clients quickly became dissatisfied with consultants who could no more than talk about e-business in the most general ways.

Nowhere was this more apparent than in the incubator market which sprang up in 1999. While some of these firms were – and remain – highly specialised, a large number positioned themselves as offering a combination of additional resources and generic business advice (on tax, legal issues, and so on). The additional resources were probably useful: talking to companies that had been through the incubation process, many acknowledged that they got more done as a result. But few of these companies had been looking for generic business advice: what they wanted was specialist knowledge – in-depth understanding of their sector, and a good network of contacts in the venture capital community that specialised in that sector. 'As a telecom venture, we needed access to telecom investors', recalled one entrepreneur. 'The list of venture capitalists drawn up by the [generic] incubator we worked with didn't have any names on it that we couldn't have written down ourselves. They were just the big names in the industry.'

From the experience of these entrepreneurs, it seems that there are two types of specialist knowledge which are particularly valued by clients:

- Industry-specific knowledge, which helps a client to identify and evaluate potential business opportunities; and
- 'Opportunity'-specific knowledge, which helps a client develop and implement an idea.

These two types of specialist knowledge also have an inverse relationship (Figure 2.2). As a new consulting market emerges, clients will be focusing on how they can apply whatever new idea has appeared to their own business and industry, but, once they've formulated some notion of what they want to do, the help required is much more around the opportunity itself – How have companies in

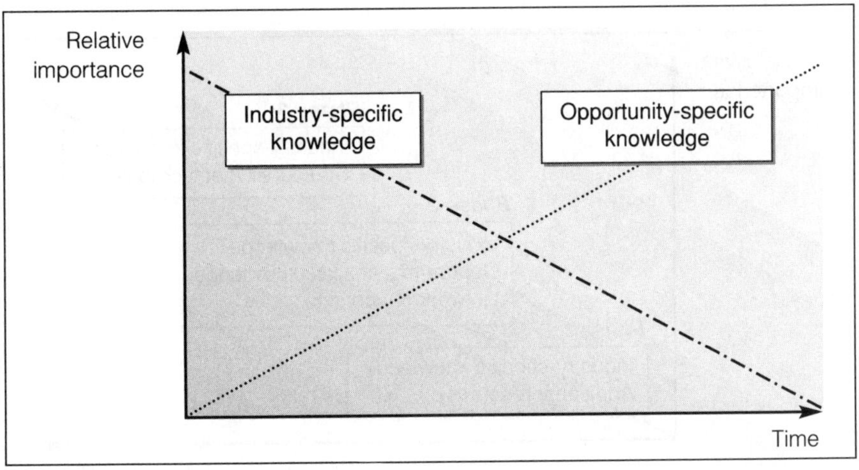

Figure 2.2 *The changing balance of industry-specific and opportunity-specific specialist knowledge*

other industries done this? What kind of benefits should they expect it to yield?

Putting all these different trends together allows us to develop a picture of how the reasons why clients hire consultants change as a market for a particular consulting service or management idea matures (Figure 2.3).

- In the first phase, the need for additional resources, new ideas and industry know-how predominates – this is the point at which clients are exploring and testing new ideas, but haven't yet settled on the way in which they will apply an idea in practice.
- The second phase is marked by a shift in which clients want to extract specific services from their consultants – in which, essentially, they know what gaps there are in their intellectual capital, and they want to fill them. In particular, they're looking to combine industry-specific knowledge, with knowledge about the opportunity they're pursuing, and they want consultants to carry out key roles in helping develop the opportunity (which, for the e-business market, took the form of helping to build a network of contacts).
- In the third phase, the need for industry-specific knowledge has been almost wholly superseded by opportunity-specific knowledge. The other need that clients are looking to satisfy is a tried-and-tested way of implementing their opportunity: their focus is now on getting to the end-game as quickly and successfully as possible.

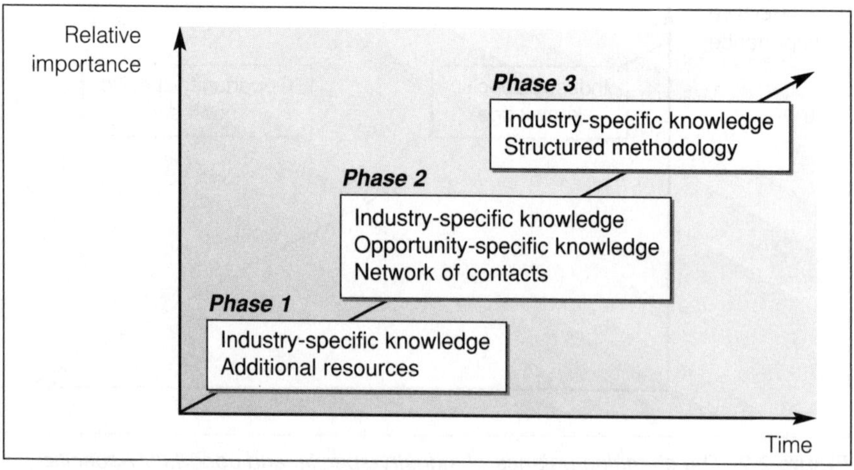

Figure 2.3 *The three-phase evolution of client needs*

So far, this analysis has focused on developing an overall picture of what happens in a consulting market – a pattern that is repeated with every new consulting service or management idea to emerge. But it can be difficult – if not dangerous – to generalise about clients in this way: after all, every client is different. What we see at the overall market level is just the summation of how individual clients are behaving: thus, in Phase 1, most – but not all clients – will fit the pattern outlined; similarly in Phases 2 and 3. While some clients evolve through the process, others may have a preferred mode of working with which they stick: thus, some clients will always be looking for industry-specific knowledge and additional resources, but others will only look for opportunity-specific knowledge and structured methodologies.

It is therefore possible to use the model outlined in Figure 2.3, not only as a means of describing the level of maturity of a market for a given consulting service, but also as a way of categorising types of clients.

- 'Phase 1' clients are companies that use consultants to explore new ideas; they primarily look to work with people who know a great deal about their sector and can, in conjunction with the client, spot and assess potential opportunities. These are the most innovative clients – the early-adopters, in effect – and are less concerned with copying what their rivals have done than in originating new thinking themselves.
- 'Phase 2' clients are those who have already identified what it is that they want to do, whether this is the implementation of a software package internally, or the launch of a new business venture. Where they need help is in bringing together the disparate skills and resources required to realise their plans – something which the speed and complexity of e-business has made even more important. 'Phase 2' clients are therefore looking for help in managing their projects: while they want a degree of industry-specific knowledge, they also need programme managers who are experienced in the particular opportunity they are pursuing and who can perform specific, quite strategic functions (in the case of e-business, help their clients identify and approach potential partners).
- 'Phase 3' clients are primarily interested in getting the job done, in catching up with what their competitors may already have

achieved. What they're looking for when they hire consultants is not innovative thinking or a long-term relationship: they need help in quite discrete areas, and they want to know that the consultants they use can almost guarantee success. Of the three types, 'Phase 3' clients are most likely to outsource a project in its entirety.

The Three Types of Client-Consultant Relationship

Both the pictures painted above – the evolution of a consulting market as a whole, and the categorisation of clients – have implications for the client-consultant relationship. From the research I've carried out over the last two years with hundreds of clients and consulting firms, three types of relationship emerge (Figure 2.4).

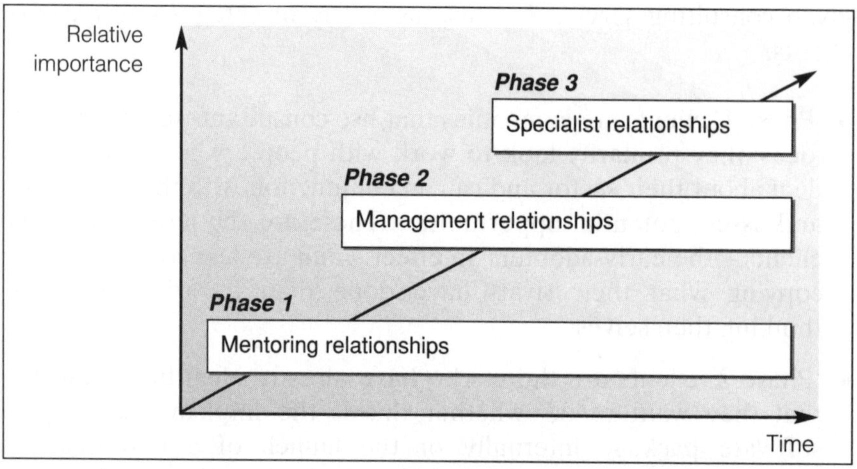

Figure 2.4 *The three-phase evolution of client-consultant relationships*

First, there are *mentoring relationships* in which the consulting firm acts as a catalyst, bringing new ideas and information, but also facilitating a client's own abilities to identify and evaluate new opportunities. Such relationships are characterised by their informality and longevity. To be successful, they require a very high level of industry-specific knowledge. However, they also often require some additional, variable resources – to help explore a promising idea in greater depth, for example. The work of the Boston Consulting Group with Delta Airlines (see Case Study 2.1) is an illustration of how a mentoring relationship works in practice.

Case Study 2.1

The Boston Consulting Group at Delta Airlines

Jim Whitehurst, a senior manager with BCG, has managed Delta's e-ventures team (staffed jointly by the airline and BCG) since its inception in January 2000. 'The main difference between the way that Delta is approaching e-business and the way in which most other airlines are going about it', he says, 'is that Delta is looking to leverage its core competencies, to use e-business as an opportunity to extend its business, not to destroy it. At Delta, the e-business management team has three roles. The first is to look at all the company's intangible assets in order to extract the maximum value from them, often by exchanging them for equity in start-ups. Delta has executed 12 such deals in total, nine since January. In the largest, Priceline, Delta received equity well before Priceline went public, for being the first major carrier to join. After Priceline went public, Delta sold shares on the open market for $784 million in cash, although it continues to hold substantial shares in the company. Obviously we have to be very careful in both tracking and valuing these assets, as the main risk for us is that we give something away for free that's potentially worth a great deal of money. Our second function, as a group, is more difficult: it involves 'deconstructing' Delta's assets into their physical and information components, identifying which among these can be exploited separately and developing a business case for doing so. Finally, we act as an internal incubator. So far, we've built one new business, a travel site – MYOBTravel.com (Mind Your Own Business Travel) – which offers the kind of travel to which large corporations generally have access, to small and medium-sized enterprises. It's an initiative that typifies Delta's overall strategy: it is good for the core, by extending the airline's relationships with small businesses and by subtly steering the airline to think more in terms of being able to offer a more personalised service to all its business customers. It also further establishes Delta's leading position in e-commerce.'

A key part to the process has been to develop a framework for thinking about assets in this way. According to Whitehurst: 'First, we needed to build a mindset throughout the company that intangible assets can be as valuable as real-world ones. We then began to think about assets along two dimensions – their uniqueness (which was generally equated with their value) and their reusability. Giving people physical space in a departures lounge is a one-shot deal, as you can't re-sell that space.

Other assets like empty seats on aircraft we generate more of daily. With these, we may build numerous partnerships, generally taking equity stakes in each. It was a structure that led us to identify assets that no one had considered before: we realised, for instance, that our key reusable asset was the time that people spend on planes. Delta's passengers clock up almost 300 million flying hours per year in aggregate. If we can generate even modest revenues from offering the ability to surf the Internet and send and receive e-mail, we can dramatically raise our net income.'

'The risk that we have to be aware of', Whitehurst says, 'is what we call "destroying option value". Too many e-business ventures are focused on the here and now, but you need to also be able to understand what options you have closed off when you go for a particular deal.'

Delta hired BCG because it wanted to get the e-ventures group up and running in a very short time frame. 'We were able to assemble a full team of e-commerce experienced professionals in a week', says Whitehurst, 'and, since then, we've been able to flex the number resources up and down depending on the workload'. This relationship – the involvement of an outside consulting firm in this very strategic role – has worked effectively because of the high degree of integration between the two sides. 'This is always a challenge and something we have to be continually aware of: we make sure that we act as a seamless unit; even though we're a mix of Delta personnel and consultants, we try to think and act as a team of Delta employees. While senior Delta officers are involved in and ultimately approve any deals we do, we are often representing Delta in the negotiation process. Our offices are at Delta, and we use Delta e-mail and voicemail.' Ensuring tight integration is critical. 'Any issues that exist between the e-ventures group and the rest of Delta are more based on the nature of what we do', he argues, 'when you've got one group of people running around, knowing things about necessarily confidential projects, which the rest of the organisation doesn't have access to. However, we continuously focus on communication and integration to ensure optimal results for Delta.'

The second type of relationship are *management relationships* in which the consulting firm's objective is to develop and implement a particular project. The emphasis here is on making things happen, as Case Study 2-2 on Cap Gemini Ernst & Young's work with the Mount Sinai NYU Health Services Organization demonstrates.

Case Study 2.2

Cap Gemini Ernst & Young and Mount Sinai NYU Health Services Organization

Darestep is the name Cap Gemini Ernst & Young has given to its user-centred solutions practice, based in newly constructed studios in the several major cities around the world, including New York and Milan. 'What we offer clients', says Mark Rankin, Darestep's global managing director, 'is a structured process designed to balance creativity with the need for swift implementation'. Darestep's approach typically begins with a three-day session in Cap Gemini Ernst & Young's Accelerated Solutions Environment (ASE), which are typically collocated with CGE&Y software development centres and DareStep studios. These sessions are often with quite large numbers of client staff, which explores the alternative strategies available to them. 'The key thing is to ensure that we have all the decision makers in the room at the same time', says Rankin. 'We want them to be able to survey the options, debate their pros and cons, but then home in on a small number of ideas that emerge from a three-step process with stages to scan the environment – focus on the client's problem at hand – and finally act through solution and project development.' From then on, clients enter a rapid process in which separate teams test the viability of each option, looking not just at the commercial potential of an idea, but the synergy between it and the client's existing business and the extent of internal change that will be required. 'It's really when a decision has been taken to focus on a particular opportunity, that Darestep really comes into its own', Rankin argues, 'because what we do is bring together a whole series of disciplines – strategy, branding, creative design, usability, content management, technology – to create a coherent user experience and integrate this into the client's existing infrastructure. We can also, if clients want us to, manage the web-site for them, which is something that is very attractive, especially where a client is uncertain of the impact of the e-venture on the way in which it does business elsewhere. Clients don't always want to start changing their customer relationship management or product development functions at a time when they're still launching a very new business. Using us means that they can effectively run two organisations in parallel.'

Rankin believes that this focused, accelerated style of approach is valuable to clients for two reasons. In the first place, he argues, it offers a multi-threaded approach. 'Serial project management won't work in this environment, not just because it's too slow, but because it tends to stack problems up to the end: you do the development work, and then you test it. That's a high-risk strategy in e-business, because you need to know what the problems are as you go along. Although we have separate teams working on different parts of a project at the same time, we bring everything together every two weeks – as though we were going to launch it – so there's continuous interaction and testing.' But, second, Rankin also believes that an important part of the value that consultants bring at this stage is in knowing how to accelerate activities without compromising the overall project: 'the uncertainty of the e-business environment – which has been exacerbated by a number of highly visible problems – means that clients find it hard to expedite their own process. As outsiders with experience in getting e-ventures to market, we can tell when the project's ready to go, even if some of the detailed tasks haven't been finished.'

Janice Weinman is the Vice President of Government Affairs, Communication and Marketing at Mount Sinai NYU Health Services Organization, a major New York health provider covering five hospitals, and has been through CGE&Y's accelerated user-centred solutions development process to build development and launch its web intiative. 'We believed that e-business represented a significant opportunity for us', says Weinman. 'We covered a multitude of different communities, internally and externally – patients, professional groups, primary care providers, suppliers, professionals interacting with patients, professionals interacting with professionals – and effective, timely and accurate communication within and between these groups is absolutely fundamental. Web-based technologies appeared to offer the chance to improve the quality of our communication in all these respects.' But the diversity of Mt Sinai's stakeholders was also a potential barrier to exploiting the new technology: it was imperative that any e-business initiative embraced the needs of all of these groups if there was to be any hope of it being adopted. CGE&Y initially helped Weinman prepare a retreat, which brought together representatives from these different groups to explore the scope and depth of the project. 'It was a microcosm of our extended organisation', Weinman recalls, 'with all the strains, challenges and politics of five merged institutions brought together in one place. People came to the meeting expecting to discuss technical issues – how a particular database could be improved, for example – but we managed to get them to go back to start from scratch, and define what they'd actually want from such a system and what we might be feasibly able to do given the budget and resources available.'

From then on, says, Weinman, the relationship with CGE&Y developed as a partnership. 'CGE&Y helped us to define the outer limits of what we could do: we'd define the components together and we'd make joint presentations to different stakeholder groups. They were also invaluable in providing a structured process which recognised our internal need for documentation without letting us get mired in bureaucracy. Although we knew from the outset that we'd need a close relationship, we were surprised by the extent to which our partnership continued to grow during the course of the project, really to the point where the client/consultant distinction had disappeared: we each knew what the other side knew; there was a lot of give and take.' Around 30 per cent of the project team came from Darestep, CGE&Y's accelerated user-centred development centre: 'but the knowledge transfer was immediate', says Weinman. 'We were living and breathing the same environment.'

Mount Sinai NYU HSO also found the clarity of thinking CGE&Y brought to be particularly valuable. 'I think the only word to describe it is "fastitidous"', says Weinman, 'every single element of the project was broken down, which meant that we were able to involve key stakeholders in specific decisions without slowing down overall progress. Because they could see the whole project, the consultants played an important role, not just in facilitating the brainstorming sessions with different stakeholder representatives, but in ensuring the internal consistency of the project as a whole.' Weinman sees this type of process as being quite different to conventional consulting: 'there was no question', she says, 'of writing a report that would gather dust on our shelves. CGE&Y recognised the urgency and were completely committed to seeing it through to fruition. It felt as though everything had been turned up a few notches.'

According to the CGE&Y's partner responsible for the Mt Sinai project, Tom Oser, making things as tangible and immediate as possible is critical in this environment: 'a 120 day delivery date is an unequivocal milestone', he says, 'and you have to have a process that creates belief in its achievability as you go along. You've got to be able to show people how the whole thing fits together and – in IT terms – you have to produce output on a regular basis. That's what makes these projects – with such ambitious time frames – so different from conventional IT projects.'

But Oser also acknowledges that another key factor in the success of Mt Sinai's project was the level of commitment and sponsorship provided by Weinman and her immediate colleagues. 'Mt Sinai recognised that there was a strategic window for this project which would close if they delayed too long. What they had was real determination to get started and a willingness to commit the necessary funds. Not all clients really have this.' Weinman agrees: 'that's where we went wrong with projects in the past – there were too many groups involved and no one was prepared to build the consensus and take the decisions required to maintain momentum'. 'In this kind of environment,' says Oser, 'communication was essential. There were so many different threads and groups involved that everything depended on there being one consistent message. Janice in particular saw this as being a key part of her role.'

Third and finally, there are *specialist relationships*. These are focused on a specific need, such as implementing a particular software package. The length of specialist relationships varies, depending on the nature of the work involved, but their success depends on in-depth knowledge of a particular issue, process or technology ('opportunity-specific knowledge'), rather than a specific industry.

While mentoring relationships will be based on trust (not least because the outputs will usually be intangible and unmeasurable), specialist relationships will be based on effectiveness (precisely because it is possible to measure whether a package has been implemented or a process completed). Management relationships will be based on a combination of both effectiveness and trust – a consulting firm is being hired because of its track record (effectiveness) and because the project manager has convinced the client that he or she is capable of delivering a successful outcome (trust). Successful mentoring relationships will be more likely to occur at an individual-to-individual level. Successful specialist relationships will be more likely to take place at an organisation-to-organisation level – for example, a client will hire a consulting firm accredited in the software they wish to implement. Successful management relationships will be forged at both the individual-to-individual level (clients need to be able to trust the individual programme manager appointed because of the stakes involved and the visibility of the project) and the organisation-to-organisation level (clients also need to be reassured that the individual in charge, however experienced and competent, is backed-up by a structured and proven methodology for delivery).

It's possible to plot these three types of relationship along these two dimensions – trust *versus* effectiveness, and the level of individual trust involved, and the balance of the three (Figure 2.5).

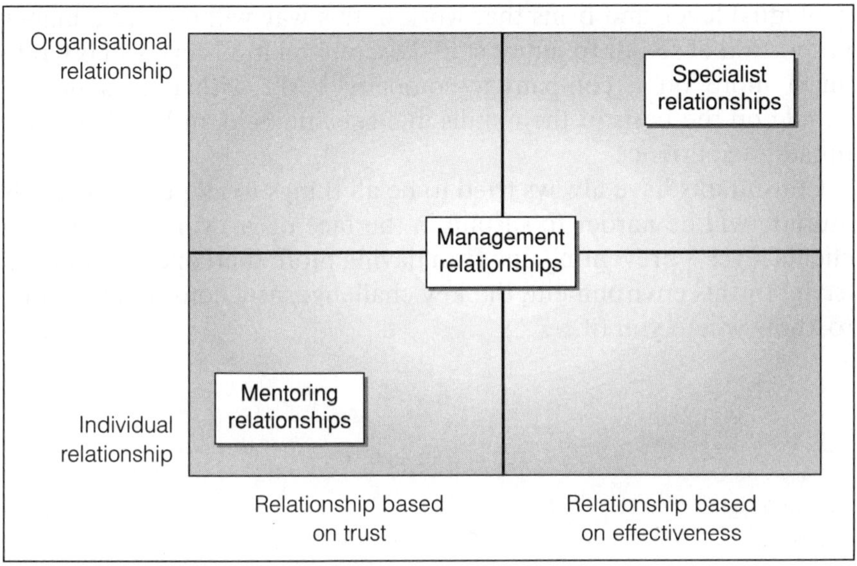

Figure 2.5 *The three styles of client-consultant relationship*

Although, at the moment, all three types of relationship co-exist, many firms are already finding that they only have one type of relationship with one client. If they work with Client A in a specialist capacity, they are highly unlikely to form a mentoring relationship with them, even though they have a mentoring relationship with Client B. Clients, far more than consulting firms, are segmenting the firms that serve them. As this effect snowballs, firms may end up in a position – only working with clients in specialist relationships, for example – from which they find it difficult to extricate themselves.

There are two factors which will constrain the ability of firms to move between relationship types in the future. First, there's the issue of objectivity: in the mentoring relationship, objectivity will be key as, without it, clients will continue to be sceptical about the motives of the consultancy involved. Clients in a mentoring relationship need to be sure that the advice they are receiving is not compromised by a firm's desire – however unintentional – to benefit financially from particular decisions about, say, the choice of technology. But objectivity will be a weakness, not a strength, when it comes to the specialist, where the discrete knowledge required will necessitate close links to specialist companies. The second factor is that the business model required to deliver each relationship effectively will be very different. Long-term relationships are likely to operate at an individual level, and firms that work in this way will require a higher proportion of senior to junior staff. Discrete relationships will operate much more on a company-to-company basis, with clients buying people on the basis of their skills in a specific field, rather than their broader experience.

Consultants have always tried to be all things to all people, but this attitude will be harder to sustain in the face of growing barriers – in clients' eyes – preventing one firm having more than one relationship 'style'. In this environment, the key challenge, as a consultant, will be to know where you fit.

3

The Consulting Industry: Segmentation and Performance

How – if at all – has e-business changed the segmentation of the consulting industry?

One of the most consistent comments made by clients in the early days of e-business was their need for the same triumvirate of skills – strategic, creative and technological – and it was in combinations of these skills that the new entrant e-specialists had found their particular and differentiating strength. However, as new economy businesses matured and as the pressure for them to deliver profits, rather than just growth, intensified, it was inevitable that their demand for additional operational and HR-related services would grow. In other words, new economy companies would start to have the same consulting requirements as old economy companies. Does this mean that after a brief blip, the consulting industry will return to where it was in 1997? Or has e-business had a more lasting impact? And, if there is an e-business legacy, how will it affect the industry in the future?

Resegmenting the Consulting Industry?

I'd argue that there have been two quite profound effects of e-business on the kinds of services offered by consultants, both of which have ramifications for how firms position themselves in the market as a whole.

Integrated working

The first was the recognition that the whole was greater than the sum of the parts – that clients obtained more value from a consulting project in which the disparate skills involved were genuinely integrated, than from a series of projects in which each skill was quite distinct. Before e-business burst upon the scene, a typical consulting project was sequential; the effect of e-business – because companies believed that the time-to-market was critical – was to compress this structure so that each stream overlapped – the 'waterfall' effect, as several people described it (see Figures 3.1a and 3.1b).

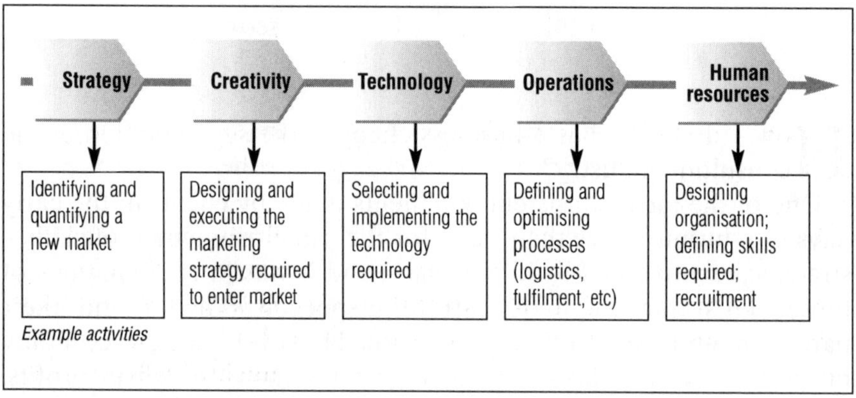

Figure 3.1a *The serial process of consulting prior to e-business*

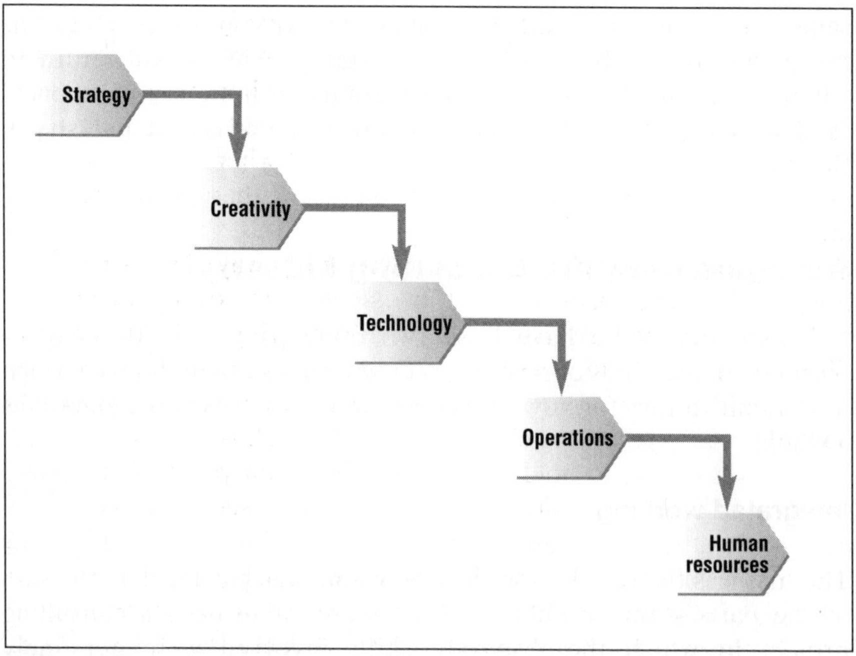

Figure 3.1b *The 'waterfall'effect of e-business on the consulting process*

The attraction to clients was – and remains – immense. Integrated teams meant shorter (although not necessarily less expensive) projects. They also meant that the perennial weak link in the consulting chain – the transition from strategy (theory) to implementation (practice) – was much less likely to be a problem: the same team that designed the strategy would be involved in executing it. Another benefit seems to have been the resulting quality of thinking. Just as companies as a whole were discovering that making links between different industry sectors could allow them to create whole new business models, so clients discovered that bringing different people and perspectives together, in an environment in which they could enhance and challenge each other's ideas, resulted in a better end product.

It's not surprising, therefore, that being able to field integrated teams was one of the key differentiators of the new entrants into the consulting market. While the established players were widely seen to have the internal divisions which prevented ideas being freely exchanged, the new firms were able to make much of their 'holistic' approach. As one partner in a new firm put it: 'we don't have a cultural legacy of rating one skill-set higher than the rest – of divisively putting our strategies above our technologists and reinforcing this message by paying them more. We can treat everyone equally, and ensure that every client team has to have a representative from each skills group.' Others took the idea further: some had all the characteristics of self-organising organisations, in which recruits could choose to which 'communities of interest' they belonged, and where standards were maintained through peer-group pressure, rather than by management intervention.

Also picking up on clients' enthusiasm for this way of working, many firms – initially, again, the new entrants – sought to position themselves as building entire businesses, rather than offering modular services. 'What we do,' said one, 'is bring everything together: we don't decouple strategy from delivery, we don't write a report and walk away. We either build an e-business with a client or we don't work with them.'

Clearly, it's easy to hold this philosophy when you're in a rapidly growing market: it's questionable whether firms, such as this one, will be able to sustain their approach during a significant downturn, that they won't be tempted to ditch their principles rather than see their revenues decline. It would also be wrong to see this mode of work as one-stop-shopping by another name. Just because clients have found integrated teams so attractive doesn't mean that they believe that the team has to come from one firm only – it's the interaction of specialist skill-sets that matters, not their provenance. In fact, some clients I talked to said quite explicitly that they'd prefer to carry the administrative and cost overhead of working with consultants from several companies than accept second-rate consultants simply for the ease of getting them from one firm.

Why is integrated working so significant for the consulting industry? Because it will increasingly cut across the internal divisions within firms, and across the external divisions between firms. Another effect will be that many of the ways we currently categorise firms will be meaningless. It won't – for instance – matter where a firm came from in the past (strategy / ex-accounting / and so on). But does this mean that segmentation becomes impossible? I'd suggest that e-business, while on the one hand it has increased the fluidity of the consulting industry, has also started to polarise it.

Proposition development *versus* enablement

One of the key things to have come out of all the conversations I've had with consulting firms over the last two years has been the extent to which firms are moving in one of two directions.

Some firms – notably some of the strategy houses and new entrants – have been aligning themselves with their clients' customers. They have been commissioning proprietary consumer research and using this as a means of gaining client attention, and have been acquiring creative agencies to strengthen their consulting offering. Typically, the work they've been doing has been focused around developing and launching a 'venture' in the broadest sense: a venture might be an e-business, spun-off from a large corporation, or it might be an internal project, where the 'customers' are actually employees. The distinctive thing about this way of working has been that it concentrates on a specific client proposition: its aim is to take this proposition to market, irrespective of whether that market is external or internal. It therefore differs from much conventional consulting work in that it is:

- Focused on the clients' end-customer, not the immediate client, in contrast to traditional consulting work, which has concentrated on the client as the means to the end;
- Aimed at delivering an end-result (increased sales if the project is external, high take-up if it is internal), rather than the means to an end result (a report, a system, and so on); and

- Involves a far higher degree of the integrated working described above.

But other firms are moving in the opposite direction: rather than work at the front-end of a new venture, they're choosing to undertake the work which 'enables' the client to launch and manage this new venture on an ongoing basis. These are the firms that are looking at logistics, fulfilment and the supply chain, at technical infrastructures and systems, and at people and processes. This type of consulting is closer to the traditional model, in that it is:

- Modular – firms can offer to deliver components, rather than complete projects; and
- Focused on the means to the end.

Each strategy has its own advantages and disadvantages. For 'proposition development' firms, the upside lies in the level of contact and influence they will have with clients – consultants who have been able to demonstrate an understanding of a client's market have always been higher up the pecking order than those that focus on the back-office activities. The fee rates, too, are likely to be higher because the work is seen to be of greater strategic importance. The downside, however, lies in the length of the projects. While the dot.com market may have collapsed, e-business has had a profound and irreversible effect on organisations' belief about the time it takes to do things: as a result, 'proposition development' projects, because they are focused on a specific proposition, are likely to be relatively short, perhaps 3–6 months, rather than 1–2 years. By contrast, 'enabling' projects may be very long: linking multiple different ERP systems isn't something you can do overnight – and the comparative longevity of enabling projects is already one of the reasons why consulting firms have been attracted to this market, even if it is at the cost of a firm's level of strategic influence with a client. The margins in this area may not be so high, but the volume of work promises to be enormous. Two dangers face enabling firms. First, there's a risk that they see 'enabling' as a means by which they can continue to offer one-stop-shopping, and that they will lose out against new, more specialist competitors, many of whom will be spin-outs from dot.coms or large corporations. Second, there's the danger that their work may become automated and thereby commoditised, much as happened to the business process re-engineering industry in the late 1990s. Without new sources of innovation and investment in specialisation, some firms may find their profits and positioning decline inexorably.

The emerging segmentation within the consulting industry

This growing polarisation – between proposition development and enablement firms – suggests that it may be a better way of segmenting the industry in the future. While it's likely that most larger firms will continue to offer some aspect of the five core consulting activities described at the start of this chapter – strategy, creativity, technology, processes and people – the balance of these services will be determined by a firm's position on the proposition development/enablement spectrum. Proposition development firms will offer strategy, creativity and some component of technology; enabling firms will focus on operations, people and – again – technology (see Figure 3.2).

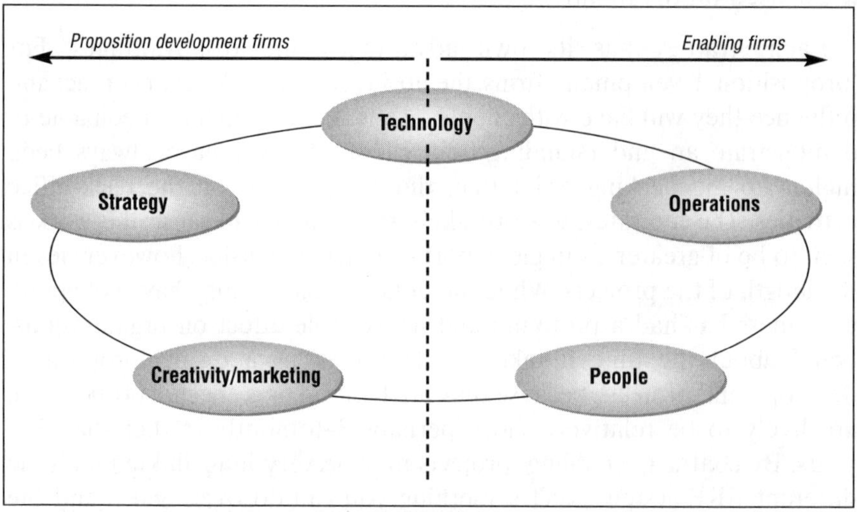

Figure 3.2 *Segmenting the consulting industry*

A further segmentation can be derived by plotting firms' positions as proposition-developers or enablers against the three types of client-consultant relationship identified in the previous chapter: mentoring relationships, management relationships and specialist relationships (Figure 3.3). Proposition development firms are most likely to work with the clients in a combination of mentoring and management roles; enabling firms in a combination of management and specialist roles. Two key points of competition emerge:

- Between proposition development and enabling firms, in terms of the management of projects; and

- Between enabling firms which offer specialist advice within their overall portfolio and a plethora of niche firms, each focusing on one particular area of specialist advice.

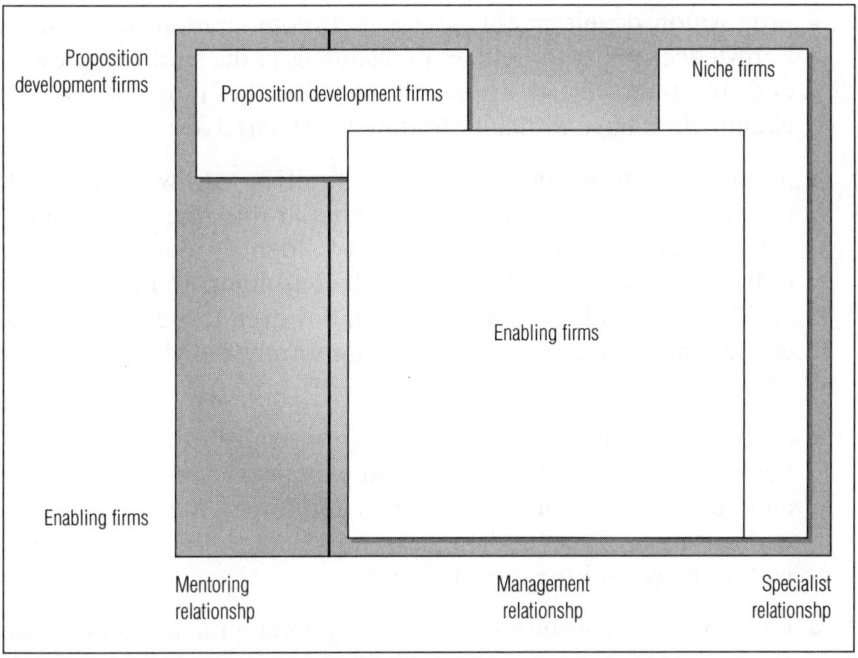

Figure 3.3 *The emerging segmentation of the consuting market*
(Note: *area indicates relative size of the market*)

By and large, it looks as though firms that carry out most of their work in the strategy and creative/marketing areas will evolve to become proposition development firms, and those focusing on technology, operations and HR will become enabling firms.

Rating the Performance of the Consulting Industry

So where, if you're a consultant, should you want to be? As noted above, each positioning has its own strengths and weaknesses, but is one approach destined to be more successful than the others?

The only way to gauge this – and we obviously can't do more than speculate at this stage – is to look at the value that clients believe consultants can add in each segment, together with the level of value added so far.

The headline messages from this research were as follows:

- The areas in which consultants are thought, by clients, to add the most value are:
  - proposition development, where their combination of specialist knowledge, ability to field extra resources at the start of a project, and tried-and-tested approach provide the momentum that clients often have difficulty finding for themselves;
  - identifying new business opportunities: it was, in fact, comparatively rare to find consultants in this role – in which a consulting firm worked with a client to identify ideas at the very outset; instead, clients tended to call consultants to help develop an idea they had already identified; however, those that did use consultants in this capacity were uniformly delighted with the results;
  - a variety of highly-specialised fields – specialist technology skills, helping in building a client's brand experience, customer service and fulfilment – something which reinforces the points made earlier about the fundamental importance of specialisation within the consulting industry; and
  - the ability of a consulting firm to bring together a disparate group of partners to participate in a client venture.
- Not surprisingly, those areas where clients thought that consultants could add least value were where a generic service was often being applied to a highly specialised sector – recruitment was one of the services which came under this heading, as was generic / strategic technology advice. Some areas – like organisational development – suffered because clients thought that the methodologies being proposed were often too old-fashioned and had not been sufficiently up-dated to take account of the new challenges of the networked economy and of boundary-less organisations.
- When it came to the reasons why clients hire consultants (see Chapter 2):
  - specialist knowledge was important in all areas of consulting work;
  - having access to a structured methodology for working was the next most significant factor, and was especially important when it

came to: identifying business opportunities, proposition development and specialist areas (technology, customer service, fulfilment, etc);

- the extent to which a firm could exploit its client base to create partnerships was another highly significant factor when it came to proposition development;
- innovative thinking was primarily important when it came to working with clients to identify new business opportunities and in terms of helping them understand their end-customers; and
- the ability to field additional resources was the least important factor, and applied largely at the start of a project or in an emerging market, and was perceived to add little value beyond that.

- The greatest gaps, between the value clients believe consultants were capable of adding, and the value that they actually felt to have been added in practice, were those relating to unspecialised areas of consulting; the overall conclusion was clear: in clients' eyes, specialised consultancy yields value, and the more specialised a consulting firm is, the more likely it is to add value. A good example of this is where consultants work with clients to help the latter understand the behaviour of their customers. While carrying out proprietary research on consumers may help position firms overall in the 'proposition development' rather than the 'enabling' camp, clients are very sceptical about the value of this research to them individually, as its regarded as being too generic to yield anything meaningful in a world that is increasingly moving towards mass-customisation and a 'segment of one'.
- There were other areas of consultancy in which the gap between perceived and actual value was smaller, but still significant: help in creating partnerships and in building the brand experience, for example. It seems likely that these markets represent significant opportunities for consulting firms, where clients believe that more can be done, but where the level of dissatisfaction is not so great as to render the market a no-go area. The potential exists, here, for a single firm to establish a more dominant position by honing its offering more effectively.

All told, the picture was one of 'good, but could do better'.

The Challenges for Consulting Firms

Part II of this book goes on to look at what 'doing better' might involve, and analyses the strategic challenges facing the consulting industry in the immediate future, in the light of the commentary in this and the preceding chapters. In some cases, this has meant re-visiting and updating points made in the original edition; in others, it has more substantial additional analysis.

- Intellectual capital – its acquisition, management, and exploitation (Chapter 4)
- Collaborative consulting – a future model for the industry (Chapter 5)
- Networking as a source of competitive advantage (Chapter 6)
- Homogeneity *versus* heterogeneity – balancing individuality with the corporate firm (Chapter 7)
- New organisational models – the impact of technology on the operations of a consulting firm (Chapter 8)
- The blurring of the boundary between clients and consultants (Chapter 9)
- Rolling out the global consulting model – a solution or an opportunity? (Chapter 10)
- Building the consulting brand experience (Chapter 11).

Part II

The Strategic Challenges

4

Intellectual Capital: Its Acquisition, Management and Exploitation

Consultancy is the application of intellectual capital from one company to another: as the previous chapter argued, clients have gaps in their intellectual capital and hire consultants to fill them. Being able to supply a never ending stream of intellectual capital is, therefore, central to a firm's ability to thrive.

Consultancy and Innovation

Yet even practising consultants, argued *Management Consultancy in the 21st Century*, admit that it is some time since their industry has been seen as a hotbed of innovation.

While noting some exceptions to this – notably the strategy consultancies – the underlying reasons were, it was suggested, economic. The consulting industry has been predicated on the fact that intellectual capital is a transferable commodity: that an assignment for one client yields commercially viable ideas, skills or processes which can be reapplied to another, even in a different sector. Without this ability to extrapolate experience or process from one company to another, from one sector to another, consultants would have nothing to sell. Moreover, because they would effectively be starting afresh with every assignment, they would have to charge clients the earth for selling it. What many of the more operationally focused consultancies excel at is in transferring 'formal' knowledge – that is, knowledge which has been codified as the result of previous assignments – from client to client. But this type of knowledge is not the same as creative thinking: in fact, consulting firms have probably spent more management time and effort trying not to 'reinvent the wheel' than they have being innovative, because the former can increase their profitability, while the latter can only reduce it. Consulting firms make money because they reapply their learning – and the more often they reapply it, the more money they earn – not from being innovative. Creativity can be dangerous.

Moreover, as the market for very large-scale consulting assignments has grown over the past ten years, the temptation to be innovative has receded further. To win and, indeed, deliver large assignments – almost all of which are implementation-focused – consulting firms have to have a track record in carrying out the complex tasks involved. Large-scale assignments are all about doing well what you have already done before. In this context, innovation is not so much irrelevant, as a positive danger. In many large and medium-sized consulting assignments, the innovative elements are confined to 'visioning workshops' and are separate from a tried-and-tested process of implementation. But this often means that the balance of the assignment is tipped in favour of the process, rather than the content of what is being done. It is therefore hardly surprising that consultancies have tended to position themselves as experts in one or other of these roles – a distinction which has been mirrored by a tendency among clients to split the two roles, bringing in different consultants for each role.

If anything, the emergence of the e-business consulting market has deepened our understanding of the powerful economic forces which serve to keep consultancy and innovation apart.

Innovation was one of the most important ways in which many of the new e-consultancies sought to differentiate themselves from established players in the consulting industry. 'Revolutions don't need consultants,' argued Neil Crofts in 1999, then head of Strategy at Razorfish, 'they need visionary leaders. We're building a quite different kind of company – we're defining our own vernacular ... which means that we should be continuously pushing back the boundaries of what is achievable within our marketspace. We don't want to become good at our jobs, in the sense of simply rolling out a familiar product time and time again. We need to be defining where the market is going.' Clients agreed: 'we brought in an e-specialist firm', said one, 'to help us develop our online business from scratch. In terms of developing our thinking, they were absolutely excellent – generating lots of challenging ideas – and we ended up with what we see as the "blueprint" for our digital business.' And the e-consulting firms were aware, too, of the poor track record of the industry when it came to sustaining any innovative input: the best had (some still have) schemes in which their consultants could take sabbaticals to develop their own ideas, organisational structures based around communities of interest rather than hierarchical status or seniority and – above all – a recognition that constant innovation meant constant change: 'we have to keep reinventing ourselves', was how one firm summed it up.

It's been a trial of strength: on the one side you have companies like Razorfish who have genuinely tried to live by their creed of innovation; but, on the other side, you have the combined weight of market conditions, client needs and shareholder demands. It's easier to be innovative in a new and expanding market: you can choose your clients, only working with those prepared to be leading edge; content (new ideas) is more important than efficient delivery (there are no benchmarks for this in any case); shareholders are more willing to tolerate losses (it's investment for the future). But there comes a time when people's patience runs out – as happened in September-October 2000 – when clients start to demand a more structured methodology (see Chapter 2) and investors, profits, and it becomes difficult to resist the temptation to take a proven approach from one client to another and to focus instead on reducing the costs of delivery.

The irony here is that, although consulting firms may be doing what clients want, they may be acting in the best interests neither of themselves or their clients. There's a small but growing body of evidence to suggest that innovation is the key to creating value for clients. Research on the impact of management thinking suggests that bandwagons occur when organisations feel pressurised into adopting a specific new idea because of the number of similar organisations that have already adopted it and irrespective of the applicability of that idea in practice:

> Bandwagon cycles can cause many organizations to adopt innovations they assess as technically inefficient. Indeed, imagine that a few organizations adopt what they assess as a technically efficient innovation that will produce profits. These adoptions initiate a bandwagon pressure. As a result, organizations that decide not to adopt the innovation because they assessed that it would yield small losses will experience an added bandwagon pressure to adopt the innovation. If some of these organizations succumb to bandwagon pressure, then the number of adopters and pressure increase further, prompting organizations that assessed the innovation as even more technically inefficient and unprofitable to jump on the bandwagon.[1]

In other words, organisations that adopt a new idea once the new idea has become established – the bandwagon has rolled – are more likely to do so because of peer-group pressure than because they are convinced of the economic value of the idea. If they had been influenced by the value of the idea, then they would have adopted it at the outset. It follows from this that the benefits of a management idea decline as its take-up grows (Figure 4.1).

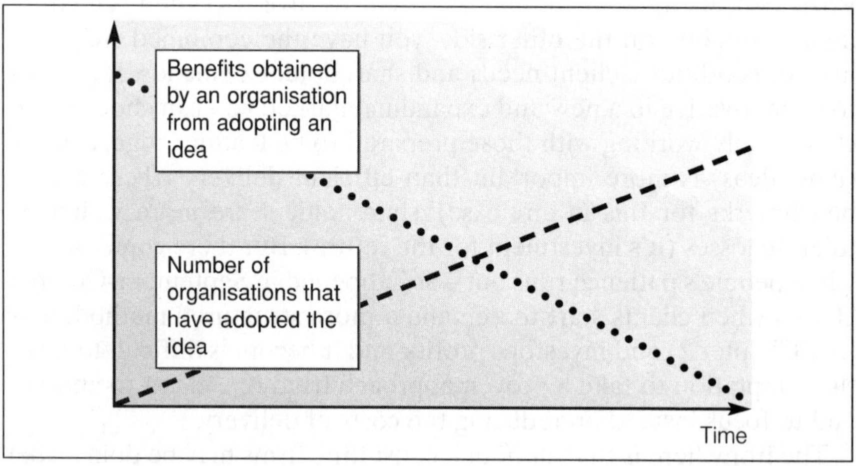

Figure 4.1 *The benefits of a management 'fad' decline as its take-up increases*

Undoubtedly, another fact in driving take-up is the level of benefits achieved by the early adopters: where these benefits appear to be very high, it's obvious that other companies will be tempted to try to replicate them. Equally, as the benefits decline, the market's enthusiasm for the idea declines.

But why should the benefits decline? The reason put forward in the academic research on this subject is essentially that late-adopters have less, in economic terms, to gain from an idea: their original rationale for rejection was sound and it is only the desire not to be seen to be missing out on something that drives them to adopt the idea later on – contrary to their better judgement. This analysis stresses the *content* of the idea, but I'd argue that it is also the *process* by which it is implemented that is significant. When an organisation identifies a new idea it believes will be beneficial, it's highly probable that it will have to work at applying that idea. The idea will still be in embryonic form; no pattern will exist for how it should be applied. I'd suggest that it's the process by which the idea is customised to a given organisation that creates value: that's why the potential value of *new* ideas is so great, and that's why *old* ideas – that have already been applied elsewhere and therefore require little in the way of customisation – are less valuable. This is essentially what happened during the business process re-engineering boom of the 1990s: the initial idea had to be highly customised to fit the first companies to use it, but thereafter, once the idea had become a standard methodology, the benefits declined. This may also be what has happened with e-business since 1998. In its earliest phase, this market spawned a whole host of new ideas, but it rapidly took on the four key attributes which characterise a consulting 'product':

- It acquire perceptible substance to it, notably in the form of business books, the written methodologies of consulting firms, and so on;
- It was heavily promoted, so that clients were aware that it existed before consultancies tried to make them buy it;
- It was articulated through its own specific language, something which gave it an identity of its own (dot.coms, hits, sticky web-sites, eyeballs, and so on); and
- It was linked – intentionally or otherwise – to wider business and cultural concerns (such as, for example, the changing demands of Generation X).

But many companies trying to enter the market later were more concerned with copying the approach of a successful rival than in analysing how the principles and technologies that underlay e-business could be applied to their own, unique circumstances. While some firms can be congratulated for helping to develop some of the most innovative ideas at the outset, many more could be criticised for persuading clients to apply them wholesale and without any degree of customisation. Indeed, you could argue that, having been slow to recognise the significance and size of the e-business consulting market, the consulting industry then reacted too fast and transformed the new ideas into standardised methodologies so efficiently and spread these methodologies from client to client so rapidly that a whole swathe of organisations, that otherwise would have remained aloof for months, if not years, was tempted to enter the e-business market. The consulting industry may have cannibalised its own market.

Avoiding a repetition of this should be high on the agenda of every consulting firm. But how to do it?

The Challenges for the Future ...

Two things hold the key to preventing the consulting industry suffering a succession of markets that – like the early stages of e-business – boom for a short period of time, only to go spectacularly bust.

Fragmenting the ideas market

One of the ways in which the consulting industry can prevent the boom-bust pattern taking hold will be to ensure that the flow of management ideas into the economy is comparatively continuous. At the moment, that flow shows every sign of becoming too consolidated. It's an unhappy truth that most managers, driven by the pressure to produce almost instant results, are on the constant look-out for potential panaceas. A herd-instinct prevails in which everyone focuses on a small number of ideas, rather than trying to develop new ones. Moreover, by facilitating the dissemination of a small number of key ideas, this is an environment which consulting firms help to create. While this may protect the profit margins of consulting firms, it does little to develop a sustainable market. In the long-run, consulting firms would do better to encourage diversity – to fragment the ideas market – so that fewer bandwagons form and so that fewer organisations adopt ideas from which they will not benefit, thus 'invalidating' the idea as well as chipping away at the reputation of consultants.

There are two strategic options: consulting firms can either become more innovative internally, or they can purchase their innovation externally.

The majority of consulting firms – large and small – have historically adopted the former approach, either by setting up specific 'R&D' groups or by trying to engender a creative environment. The 'skunk group' approach has the advantage that it allows people the opportunity to think creatively, without also having to worry about maintaining billable hours. It also allows the consulting firm to ring-fence the creative activity so that it does not interfere with its mainstream operations – delivering formalised knowledge to clients. But a knock-on effect is to make it difficult to integrate any of the creative thinking back into the mainstream practice: in other words, being innovative remains at best a marginal activity. Developing a creative environment might resolve this issue – although it might also, for that reason, pose a threat to the profitability of the consultancy. If everyone is going around creating new ideas, then who is responsible for bringing in any sustainable profits? Moreover, 'being creative' as a strategy may work effectively for smaller consultancies, whose organisation is probably more flexible and who are culturally happier to take risks, but it may well be impossible for the larger, more established firms, most of whose culture is built around successful – low-risk – approaches to delivery.

Faced with obstacles to generating ideas internally, it seems likely that some consulting firms in the future will turn to the second option – acquiring new ideas externally. This is, after all, just a more extreme and visible version of what happens already. Consulting firms complain a great deal about the lack of potential recruits for their industry, a problem caused as much by their high staff turnover rates (often up to 25 per cent per year) as it is by changes in demographics or educational standards. New recruits are currently the means by which consulting firms acquire new intellectual capital. With the shift – in most firms – away from graduate recruitment, consultancies are increasingly looking for people who have skills, experience and ideas; who can demonstrate the implementation of ideas in their organisations. Once the recruit has joined, his or her ideas are incorporated into proposals and assignments, gradually being subsumed into – and also refreshing – the collective intellectual capital of the firm. However, this strategy has its weaknesses. First, consultancy companies are running out of new recruits (an issue which is covered in more detail later); thus, the conventional well of ideas is beginning to run dry. Second, even if a consulting firm could recruit all the people that it needed (to carry out billable work), then this might not meet its requirements for new ideas. If it recruited enough people to supply the ideas it wanted, then the firm might well end up with more people than it could actually occupy on billable work.

The answer to this dilemma – although it goes against the grain of much consultancy thinking – will be to divorce the idea from the person. Thus, rather than recruit a person to get an idea, the consulting firm will simply buy the idea and sell it to clients, probably in the meantime hiring someone else to deliver the idea. This distinction between idea and person has several advantages. Clearly, it means that the consulting firm is not burdened with an additional member of staff, whose skills as a consultant may be limited. But, more importantly, it also allows the consulting firm to maintain the distinction between creativity and delivery on which much of its internal operations and profitability is dependent.

Indeed, the seeds of this trend are already apparent. The links between business schools and consultancies are becoming closer and more numerous. It also seems likely that consulting firms will hire management gurus as associate partners. Ironically, they will be outsourcing the development of their intellectual capital to academics and specialists, just as many clients have already outsourced the development of their intellectual capital to consultancies. To meet clients' needs to have more new ideas, consultancies will, in effect, be setting up back-to-back agreements with their suppliers of intellectual capital, ones which guarantee a certain number of ideas, probably at a prespecified price and delivered at a specified time (because one of the problems consultancies have encountered with internal innovation is that its costs and delivery dates are notoriously uncertain). Although such 'contracts' will essentially be invisible from the client's viewpoint, the role of the consultant will have changed from being a manufacturer of new ideas, to an intermediary – a conduit of ideas to their clients – reliant on other companies, institutions or individuals finding and supplying them with those ideas. At the moment, most consulting firms head-hunt for new recruits: in the future, they look set to head-hunt for the best ideas.

Separating the individual from the idea

The other key challenge is the efficiency with which consulting firms can convert their ideas into sellable products – their intellectual capital into intellectual income. If the e-business consulting market is anything to go by, then this would appear to be a challenge to which consultants have risen. Indeed, they have almost become victims of their own success, with ideas being 'methodologised' before they've been fully developed. Once again, the economic pressure to find a way of delivering even the newest ideas profitably has overwhelmed any desire to retain an innovative, even highly-customised, approach. Of course, it's not just the consulting industry which has been at fault here: the whole pressure to develop methodologies is driven by clients who want to purchase something tangible with a high guarantee of success, and by investors or partners unwilling to accept lower levels of profitability than those to which the industry has been accustomed.

It's delivery here that is the underlying problem: the real challenge over the next few years is for consultants to be able to deliver innovative products and services as efficiently as they deliver standardised ones.

But can they do this? For all the investment in knowledge management systems by consulting firms over the last few years, progress seems to have been slight. Perhaps the main stumbling block is a conceptual one: the key to the industry's prevailing inefficiency is its reliance on individuals to be innovative. To change the underlying economics, consulting firms will have to divorce ideas from the heads that conceive them. This is borne out when we look at how some of the new entrant consulting firms managed to expand so very rapidly in the late 1990s. One of their distinguishing features was the extent to which they managed this migration from being a collection of professionals to being an entity with collective assets without compromising the creativity of individual employees. 'We're obsessed with the process of creative destruction,' said one such firm: 'the best way of renewing ourselves is to change constantly the way we do things'. But these firms also recognised that culture needs to be sustained by a 'hard' infrastructure: knowledge management systems, methodologies and performance measurements which ensure that the company builds up the collective intellectual assets that enable it to innovate on a systematic basis, rather than wholly relying on specific individuals to be innovative. 'Perhaps the biggest change for us internally', acknowledged an established firm I interviewed, 'has been to our knowledge network'.

E-business required consulting firms to take a more proactive, less opportunistic approach to gathering, analysing and valuing their knowledge – and this will continue to be the case in the foreseeable future. It will be a matter of survival: clients have too many other sources of information to be interested in anything other than in-depth analysis (as investment banks are finding to their cost) – and in-depth analysis cannot be created instantly, but requires long-term investment and dedicated resources. Consulting firms will need to assess their intellectual assets on a regular basis in order to identify future services. The potential value of these could then be quantified more systematically in terms of their market value, rather than on the time likely to be spent delivering them. Moreover, moving from seeing knowledge as a homogeneous entity to a portfolio of different service 'packages' (high/low return, large/small market, long/short shelf life) will prompt consultancies to invest differently.

The key here will be to separate knowledge from the people who know. You can't value, sell effectively or protect ideas that are in people's heads; but you can do all of these things, if you treat knowledge as a distinct entity, and one which is the combined fruit of many people and much research, rather than the personal skills and experience of a specific individual. But this is something consultancies find particularly hard, as they continue to see themselves as 'people businesses'. Moving away from this sense of identify threatens their self-image. For all the slump in their stocks, this continues to be an area where the new entrant e-consulting specialists have an advantage. Theirs has been a more corporate approach than has traditionally been the case in the consulting industry, but it is also one that is comparatively untroubled by the belief that constrains most incumbent firms – that this approach can only be pursued at the expense of individual autonomy and creativity.

The challenge for these firms will be retaining the initiative. The consulting industry has not suffered the individual/corporate dichotomy from choice, but because its underlying economics make polarisation virtually inevitable. Conflicting pressures exist, pushing firms, on the one hand, to fragment (because the value of individual expertise has made the collective entity redundant) and, on the other, to merge (in order to achieve economies of scale by sacrificing individual innovation to the profitability of the whole). The new entrants have still to demonstrate that they can withstand these pressures.

... and the Threats

A key treat to the consulting industry is that management ideas are increasingly (and increasingly rapidly) converted into software.

Traditional consulting has delivered highly tailored services with minimal efficiency – the modern equivalent of an eighteenth-century craftsman producing a Chippendale chair. The quality is usually high, but the process of producing it is slow because the skills involved cannot be automated. Prior to the increased competition of the late 1980s, efficiency was not an issue, due to the high fees which consultants were able to charge. As competitive pressures have grown, the established consulting firms have all made efforts to increase efficiency, with varying degrees of success; overall, however, the nature of consulting has made it difficult for consulting services to be mass-produced. The antithesis of this is the software industry. Once the initial – and considerable – investment has been made in developing the software, the final product can be mass-produced in almost no time and at almost no cost. Yet consultants and software packages effectively fulfil the same function, although they do it by very different means. They both allow clients/users to do things that they could not otherwise have done, by filling gaps in their intellectual capital. Consultants do this by bring new ideas and skills to bear on their clients' problems; software, by providing tools (and – with CD-ROM databases and the Internet – increasingly knowledge) to which their users would not otherwise have access. From this perspective, software poses one of the biggest threats to traditional consultancy in the future. In fact, software's erosion of conventional consulting markets can already be seen in the tax advisory market. A decade ago, clients might have called in a tax adviser to help out with the tax computation, a function now performed by tax software packages. Tax consulting has, as a result, moved further up the advisory food-chain – offering increasingly strategic tax planning ideas – but software continues to snap at its heels in the form of increasingly sophisticated tax management tools. How long can the tax consultant manage to stay ahead?

It is comparatively easy for software manufacturers to encroach on tax advisory work because the latter is already neatly 'packaged' for consumption, if only because it has to be directed towards certain common problems. Because it is 'pre-packaged', the process of converting the tax consultant's intellectual capital into a series of rules, and thence into a computer program, can be very fast. By contrast, management consultancy, precisely because it is conventionally tailored to individual client needs, has been more difficult to codify. But, in a world in which consulting firms are trying to produce many more ideas and to convert them into tangible 'products' from a client's perspective, the division between management consultancy and software will be less clear-cut. As consulting firms produce more 'products', so will they provide software companies with the starting point of a new software package. Once again, there is some evidence that this is already happening to a limited extent. A few years ago, you might have sent your staff on a time management course (perhaps you still do), but many of the skills taught on these courses are now embodied in time management packages. It seems likely that, if a technique like business process re-engineering were to be invented in ten years' time (and, undoubtedly, something along these lines will be), then at least part of the consulting service – perhaps even all of it – will be based around a software package.

Given client demands for more and more concrete consulting services, it seems inevitable that the distinction between consultancy advice and software will be less clear. Software, after all, offers consulting firms the solution to both problems – speed and tangibility. However, it also poses a considerable threat. If all that consultancies are going to do in the future is churn out new, packaged ideas, how long will it take for them to be perceived to be commodity producers, much like software manufacturers? This is the Catch-22 of clients' simultaneous demands for speed and tangibility. In an ideal world, consultants need to move from producing tailored but inefficient services – the Chippendale chair-maker – to producing tailored but efficient services (Figure 4.2). The danger is that they will not be able to make the move from inefficiency to efficiency, without also moving from a tailored product to a standardised product – the software manufacturer. But, if their clients want to have their cake and eat it, consulting firms are going to need to square this particular circle.

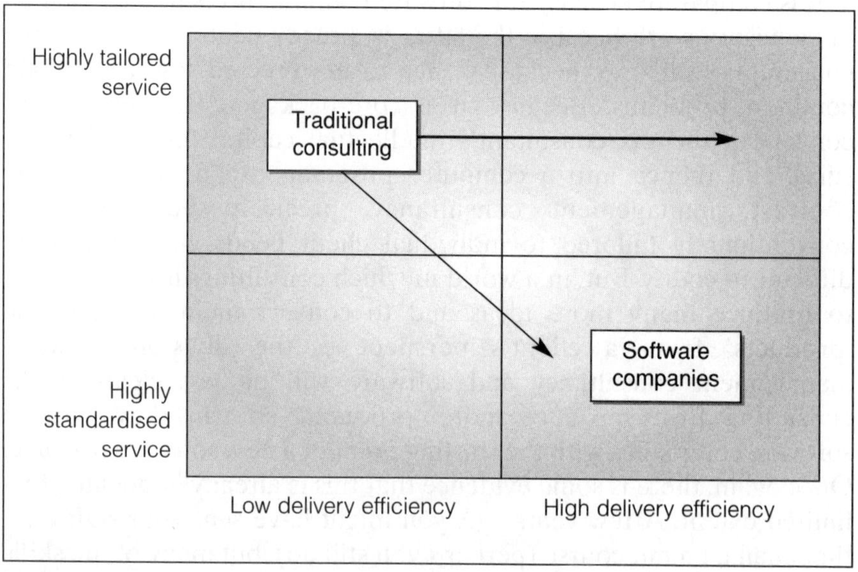

Figure 4.2 *Two evolutionary paths for the consulting industry*

At the moment, a consulting product succeeds or fails depending on the extent to which it accidentally exploits one or more of these features. In the future, as clients demand an increasing number of new ideas, each of these four attributes will need to be developed consciously and systematically – something which has significant operational implications for consulting firms, most of which do not, as we noted earlier, have a good track record for innovation on a commercially viable basis.

[1] Eric Abrahamson and Lori Rosenkopf, 'Institutional and Competitive Bandwagons: Using Mathematical Modeling as a Tool to Explore Innovation Diffusion', *Academy of Management Review*, 18:3 (July 1993), p. 487.

5

Knowledge Sharing: The Case for Collaborative Consulting

In *Intelligent Enterprise*, American academic James Brian Quinn argues that 'the common element among [professional service organisations] and industries is the predominance of managing intellect – rather than managing things – in creating their value added.'[1] Unlike manufacturing companies that can rely on unique products or technologies, conventional wisdom has it that consulting firms gain competitive advantage largely through their ability to make use of proprietary knowledge. Indeed, access to and ownership of intellectual capital remain, as Chapter 4 reinforced, central to a consulting firm's success.

Several factors have been driving consulting firms to invest in managing their intellectual assets more effectively: the need to eradicate operational inefficiencies; the availability of knowledge management technology; the fact that many clients have been making similar investments; and the need for consulting firms to strengthen their credibility by being able to demonstrate 'codified' knowledge.

In *Management Consultancy in the 21st Century* I suggested that there were two factors which could make the future of knowledge management significantly different to its past, or even its present: first, that clients are demanding more ideas more quickly; second, that knowledge management will become a means – not so much to be a leading player in the consulting market – but to survive. To demonstrate this, I took an example of two hypothetical consulting companies. Both companies had knowledge management systems, both were working on similar projects (in this case, cutting the cost of research and development in the pharmaceutical industry). Both drew on previous work in the sector to do this, but Company A did so more efficiently than Company B, allowing it to complete its assignment first. Moreover, Company A was also both more efficient and more effective at taking the output from this assignment and incorporating it in its knowledge management system, making it rapidly available for use with other clients. This means that when the two companies next competed for a similar piece of work, Company A had an advantage – a better body of knowledge to draw on. And each time Company A beat its rival – as it would do more and more, as its advantage grew – it built up its base of knowledge, further increasing its chances of continuing to win work in the future. A virtuous circle was created, in which Company A's critical mass of knowledge attracted additional knowledge, thus constantly strengthening Company A's competitive advantage. Ultimately, Company B would be pushed out of this particular market. Replicate this across multiple markets, and Company B would go out of business.

The practical example I quoted was of ERP-related consultancy, where a sizeable and quite distinct market emerged in the early 1990s. From the perspective of consulting firms, ERP related consultancy was an object lesson in the importance of establishing early footholds in new knowledge markets as they emerge. As the market for ERP consultancy suddenly burgeoned, only a minority of consulting firms recognised the potential. Those that did were quick to recruit the few trained ERP consultants available and to win assignments with clients which helped them to build up critical mass, in terms of both numbers of people and intellectual capital. By the time the second wave of entrants had materialised, the first-wave companies had already established a hold on the market which was difficult to break. In an almost textbook example of the idea of 'increasing returns' within the economy[2], those firms with ERP expertise went from strength to strength, effectively creating knowledge-based barriers to entry, even in a market where demand continues to outstrip supply.

It's a scenario that clearly haunted many of the larger, established consulting firms as the e-business emerged in 1998–99. 'When companies like SAP grew so rapidly, we were really just spectators', said one consultant I talked to. 'Yes, we earned plenty of money in terms of fees, but we didn't have the almost exponential growth that the company itself enjoyed.' Determined to avoid this mistake again, such firms looked to invest in the SAPs of the future: knowledge was a landscape in which consulting firms had to stake their claim, or see their position marginalised.

But even this may not be enough. We're used to thinking of ownership and access as being ends in themselves, but they may prove to be simply a means on the way to a more important end. Greater distinction between firms' intellectual assets clears the way to a more collaborative way of working. To understand the significance of this, we have first to look at the way in which the intellectual value chain of the consulting industry is changing.

The Intellectual Value-Chain

One of the important effects of e-business has been to make us more conscious of the role that information plays in the economy. According to Philip Evans and Thomas Wurster in *Blown to Bits*:

> corporations ... ally with each other to form the supply chains that define an industry. Supply chains link supplier and customer corporations together. They are shaped by the same kind of informational logic as the value chains within companies but in a weaker form. When two companies build a long-term relationship, they establish channels for the rich communication of information. These channels may be personal acquaintances among executives or sales and purchasing staff.... mutual understandings that are implicit or written into contracts .... all, in different ways, are information channels ... Information is the glue that holds value chains and supply chains together. But that glue is now melting. The fundamental cause is the explosion in connectivity and in the information standards that are enabling the open and almost cost-free exchange of a widening universe of rich information. When everyone can communicate richly with everyone else, the narrow communications channels that used to tie people together simply become obsolete. And so do all the business structures that created those channels or exploit them for competitive advantage.[3]

This is precisely what is happening in the consulting industry. There are four essential stages by which consultants create economic value for their clients, each of which have specific types of intellectual capital associated with them (Figure 5.1).

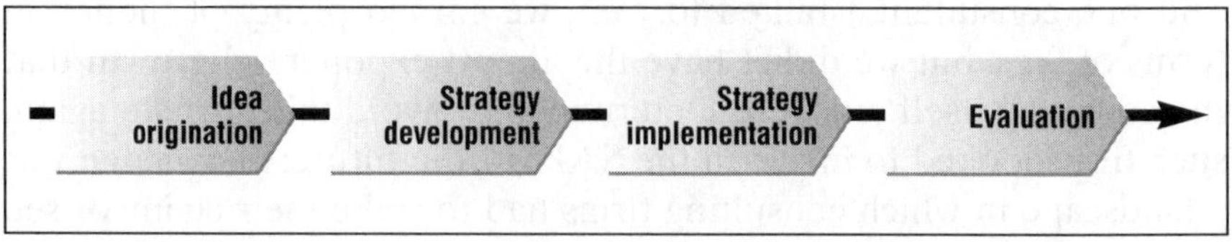

Figure 5.1 *The intellectual value-chain of the consulting industry*

Historically, consulting firms have been the creators – and thus the owners – of these different types of intellectual capital: they gathered the market data, identified trends within it, recommended strategies, selected software packages, and so on. But clients today have alternative routes of gaining information – directly from the Internet, commissioned from market research companies or business schools; some of that information comes 'pre-digested' – marketing packages can assess the effectiveness of web-based initiatives by monitoring users behaviour automatically. Really, the only area in which consultants continue to hold sway is in the application of human thought to that information (in effect, knowledge), and it's questionable how long this will continue unchallenged: as clients improve their direct access to information and data, it's highly likely that they will build up the expertise required to carry out the interpretation itself, and will thus begin to compete with consultants on their home ground.[4]

Moreover, without exclusive ownership of the sources of data and information, consultants will find it increasingly hard to sustain client relationships through all four stages in the value chain. In one sense, this has always been a difficulty for consultants: the gaps between stages – particularly that between strategy development and implementation – have always been weak links in the consulting process, and many a engagement has failed because it has not been possible – for example – to translate a strategic idea into a workable reality. But e-business has made a difficult situation even worse: by increasing clients' demand for specialist knowledge and by opening up many new, more fragmented sources of specialist data and information, e-business has made it hard for any one firm to be knowledgeable in all parts of the value chain. For all the talk in the late 1990s about e-business requiring a more holistic approach to consulting, the reality is that strategy and implementation expertise are even further apart than before.

Fragmentation and Disintermediation

For consulting firms that aspire to be the panacea of all their clients' ills – one-stop-shops in the parlance of the industry – such developments are decidedly threatening.

As the consulting industry – as I think it will – fragments over the next 2–5 years, in response to the twin pressures of client demand for greater specialisation and the disintegration of the intellectual value chain, it may begin to look more like the film industry (Figure 5.2). A studio has an option on a particular idea; it discusses it on and off with a small number of executive producers with whom the studio has worked in the past, and at some point decides to make the film. A producer is hired, who, in conjunction with the studio and the executive producer, appoints a director. While the director then takes charge of hiring the cast and filming, the producer pulls together the highly complex logistics that go into film making – hiring the crew, finding the locations, building the sets, and so on – as well as keeping control of the overall timetable and budget. The key feature about the way in which the film industry works is that a multitude of independent specialists come together for a short period of time, with a specific goal (making a film); some of these specialists play a very specific role and are only involved for a very short period; others – like the director and producers – are involved from start to finish. Once the film is completed, the crew disbands.

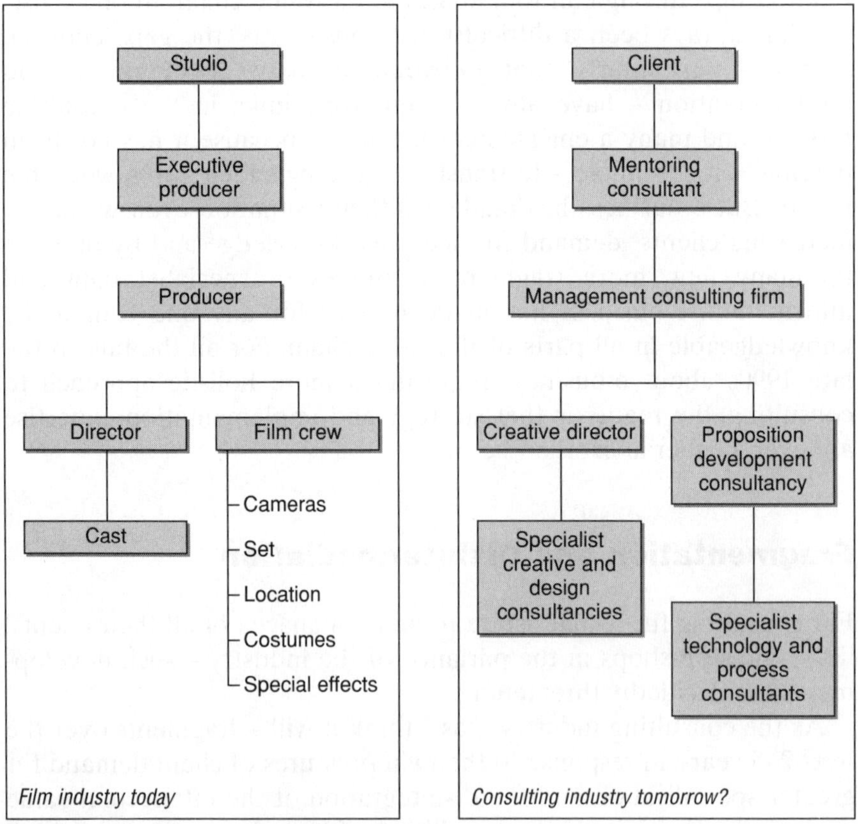

Figure 5.2 *The consulting industry as film production*

The 'incubator' style of working is significant because it introduced film industry-like methods into the consulting industry. A client (the studio) has an idea: it may brainstorm that idea with a small number of consultants with whom it has a long-term relationship, and then hires a consulting firm to manage the development of the venture; this firm, in turn, orchestrates a whole host of specialist firms, each with a specific role.

Historically, the single most important difference between the film and the consulting industry is that films are created by a large number of very small companies and freelance specialists, whereas consulting projects have tended to be delivered by a single firm, calling on the varied resources of its worldwide network. This has already started to change, with consulting firms increasingly finding themselves in the role of doing prime-contracting, co-ordinating work with firms they would otherwise regard as competitors, but this style of working is likely to increase exponentially, faced with the dual pressure of e-business – complexity of projects and the perceived need among clients for specialist resources. Collaborative consulting has begun.

For the consulting industry to work in a structure not dissimilar to that of the film industry requires three things to happen:

- Consultancies need to know where they fit into the more complex value chain;
- Consulting projects need to be more visible; and
- Clients need to have access to the information required to assemble project teams.

Knowing where they fit in

It's one of the recurring irritations of the consulting industry that the vast majority of firms who have expanded beyond the niche on which they were originally focused remain unclear about the precise nature of their intellectual capital. As one client I recently interviewed put it: 'One of the main problems with the consulting industry is that people – clients and consultants alike – don't tend to think in terms of pure intellectual capital. The traditional unit in which you buy consultancy is people, and it's therefore hard to separate people from ideas. In fact, consultants make this even harder by being bad at articulating their knowledge proposition. What clients need to be able to do is to define precisely the intellectual capital they need and to be able to match this against the intellectual capital on offer from a given set of firms.'

It's still the case that only a tiny minority of consulting firms have anything like a comprehensive understanding of their intellectual assets. For new, small or highly homogeneous companies, there will be an intuitive sense of what these assets are, but for the more diverse, long-standing companies, the gap between what they know they have and what they actually have is immense. In most of this second type of firm, intellectual capital only becomes visible when it is written up as a case study of an assignment or when it is converted into more general application, perhaps in the form of a marketing brochure. This inevitably means that much of a firm's true intellectual capital never gets out of the head of the consultant who thought of it. To combat this problem, many firms have recognised the need to appoint support staff who are responsible for going from consultant to consultant, assignment to assignment, in order to gather and record intellectual capital which could be exploited by other parts of the organisation. This is, however, an essentially bottom-up approach and one which is unlikely to yield 'big' ideas.

For consulting firms to be able to understand their position in the remodelled intellectual value chain, they will need to carry out top-down audits of their intellectual capital on a more formal basis, just as a decade ago they might have been investing in a registry of physical assets.

Making projects more visible

One of the key differences between the film and consulting industries is the profile of their output. In fact, it's hard to imagine two outputs more different. A film is publicised, it's highly visible, and every contributor – from the $1 million a day diva to the animal trainer – gets a mention at the end. By contrast, a consulting project has typically been something that happened behind the scenes, cloaked in the mystique the industry has gathered around it. Most importantly, consultants have played the part of facilitators, not prime movers: the credit (and the blame) is all the clients'.

But the consulting-project-as-film analogy will only work if consultants can feel confident that they will be given their due – that, when a project is successful, potential clients can be made aware of the firm's contribution. Where consultants remain anonymous, they are dependent on their input to the process (their brand), rather than their output (the results of the project).

Two factors are changing this – and this is another area in which e-business has had a significant impact.

First, nothing has been as fast a means of gaining credibility as being able to say to clients 'we did that', and consultants have, for the first time, been coming out of the wings to take a bow. Credibility has become a critical 'must-have' when clients are buying consultancy, especially where, as was the case with e-business consulting in 1998–99, the market is a barely emerging one and where levels of uncertainty are high. Having found that taking public credit for successful projects represents a fast track to gaining credibility in this instance, consulting firms are likely to repeat the strategy when it comes to the next management bandwagon.

Second, getting consultants to publicly ally themselves to specific ventures has advantages in clients' eyes as well. For decades, clients have been frustrated in their attempts to make consulting firms accountable for their actions: consultants have claimed many factors – the number of variables that affect outcome, changing market conditions, the client's role in implementation, but, ultimately, the confidentiality of the client-consultant relationship – to avoid being held responsible for what happens. An environment in which consultants accept credit (and therefore can be attributed with blame) goes some way to resolving this issue.

Information to navigate

The only reason why the idea of a one-stop-shop continues to have any value whatsoever in the consulting industry is that it is currently the primary mechanism by which clients can identify specialists across the world. Consulting firms have a monopoly of knowledge about themselves: that's enormously valuable information and it's the reason why there's hardly a single larger firm that makes its telephone directory available to the public. After all, what value is the collective firm adding to its clients? The comments of one sum up the thoughts of many: 'the power of these firms essentially lies in the networks they own. If I want to reach the global expert in a specific area in a Big Five firm, I need help finding my way through all the possible options. But, once I've identified the people with whom I want to work, the firm as a whole doesn't have a great deal to add.'

A consulting firm is essentially an intermediary, helping clients identify the right person or group of people with whom to work. Over the years, consulting firms have – like other intermediaries – tried to strengthen the hold they have over their clients by incorporating additional facets designed to increase loyalty: quality assurance procedures aimed at raising the overall standard of engagement delivery; links to other organisations that reduce a client's incentive to look elsewhere for assistance; knowledge networks that enable a single consultant to bring the global brain of the organisation to bear on the problems of a local client.

At present, the consulting industry could not run along the lines of the film industry – as suggested here – because there is insufficient information available to enable clients to identify these specialists for themselves.

However, if we've learnt one lesson from e-business so far, it's that the position of intermediaries is very precarious. There are plenty of other sources of knowledge becoming available, and some web-sites already exist that are designed to help companies select consulting firms, although these are largely aimed at small to medium sized businesses and freelance consultants, rather than at large corporations or established consulting firms.

There are good economic reasons to believe that even the largest consulting firms will be disintermediated in the end. Like other intermediaries, consulting firms earn their keep by charging a premium for their navigation services, and the opportunity exists for someone – not necessarily a consulting firm – to offer an equivalent service, either for a lower price or even, potentially, free of charge. There are companies out there that are already positioning themselves as navigation specialists: what's to prevent them from offering advice on, for example, financial services consultants to complement the financial information they're already providing. The technology exists to make the process of navigating through a consulting firm much less painful than many clients seem to find it at present. It could also make a great deal of sense to bundle consulting-related information up with other specialist sources of data. Even the role that the consulting firm has in 'guaranteeing' a certain level of quality could be challenged – perhaps by an Internet-based company that collates feedback and recommendations directly from clients themselves.

Of course, collaboration will not stop with consulting firms. The combined effect of consultants working together and clients' awareness of their own intellectual capital resources (discussed in Chapter 2), means that it will become impractical – if not impossible and undesirable – to draw a distinction between client and consultant 'participants'. This, in turn, is likely to change the nature of the role each party plays: clients will be there to give advice as well as learn; consultants will be there to learn as well as give advice. They will genuinely become partners (a word which has otherwise been extensively mis-used by the consulting industry to cover any time of contractual arrangement in which the consultant does more than simply tell the client what to do next).

---

1 James Brian Quinn, *Intelligent Enterprise: A New Paradigm for a New Era* (New York: Free Press, 1992)

2 See W Brian Arthur, 'Increasing Returns and the New World of Business', *Harvard Business Review*, July–August, 1996.

3 Philip Evans and Thomas S Wurster, *Blown to Bits: How the New Economics of Information Transforms Strategy* (Cambridge MA: Harvard Business School Press), p.13.

4 I am indebted to Terry McGrath at McCann-Erikson in London for her work on how information is changing the value chain within the advertising industry.

6

Consulting in the Networked Economy

The previous chapter made a case for consulting firms working together more closely than ever before. But collaboration will not – I'd argue – stop at the conventional boundaries of the consulting industry: once the principle's established, there's little to stop consultants collaborating with clients and *vice versa* – indeed, they are already doing so.

Why? Because collaboration doesn't just hold the key to improved client service (by integrating specialist skills) or increased profitability (by enabling firms to shed their less successful services: it will also be a factor in determining future growth.

Consulting firms have never really diversified. Obviously, they've expanded into new consulting markets in response to client needs and the late 1990s did see a spate of acquisitions and alliances with other types of professional service firms, but consultants have never really operated outside the professional service sphere. The essential reasons for this are economic: organisations diversify when they want either to grow (where their current markets are saturated), or to improve their profitability (where their current margins are constrained) or to out-manoeuvre potential new entrants (where their core market is under threat). The almost continuous expansion of the consulting market since the Second World War has meant that growth has always been forthcoming within the consulting market itself: firms have had no reason to move outside it. While new entrants have emerged, these have been neither so numerous nor so aggressive to have any substantial impact on the industry as a whole. But e-business changed this, in three ways. First, it showed that the profitability of the consulting industry, while still high in comparison to many other sectors, was completely outpaced when it came to sectors – notably software development – where the costs of delivery were virtually zero. Second, it was accompanied by a massive wave of new entrants (start-ups and companies spun out of existing corporations), to the point where there is now significant over-capacity in the consulting industry. Finally, it made clear how a tangible component to a business (customer relationships, software, and so on) was central to having a sustainable competitive advantage. If consulting firms were to secure their future – it was realised – they might well have to break the habit of a generation – and diversify.

The Growing Importance of Networking

Although *Management Consultancy in the 21st Century* never mentioned 'e-business', it did stress the growing importance of inter-company co-operation in helping companies diversify. Although alliances and mergers, it pointed out, have been part and parcel of business, what was new was that these were now happening across traditional sector boundaries. Rather than solidifying existing industry structures, these alliances were creating new industries, straddling different parts of the conventional value chain. Instead of looking to ally with organisations for the purposes of vertical integration, companies are looking either to make alliances across the value chain, or to by-pass traditional links in the value chain. *Management Consultancy in the 21st Century* also argued that the nature of competition appeared to be changing as a result of the alliances being formed. There has always been a paradoxical relationship between collaboration and competition. In theory, collaboration will increase an organisation's ability to compete (because it strengthens its core competencies), but at the same time, collaboration (especially among companies in the same sector) reduces the need for direct competition. But this, as US academic Benjamin Gomes-Casseres pointed out in 1997, was changing:

> In the modern world of large firms, global businesses, and advanced technologies, the relationship between these two processes is much more complex. The type of business rivalry emerging in this environment grows out of the very dynamics of collaboration. Simply put, business rivalry now often takes place between sets of allied firms, rather than between single firms.[1]

However, much of what *Management Consultancy in the 21st Century* had to say about the applicability of this theory to the consulting industry was speculative. Although there was plenty of merger and acquisition activity in the sector, most of it followed conventional patterns, focusing on vertical integration, primarily between consultancies and software companies.

One of the most important effects of e-business on the consulting industry has been to make the economic rationale for diversification much more compelling. Looking in detail now at the points mentioned above:

- *Growth:* Most of the larger, established consulting firms have been growing at rates between 15 and 25 per cent since the mid-1990s. The e-consulting specialists, launched in the late 1990s, grew far more rapidly – far more rapidly, indeed, than any set of new entrants had managed in the past. In 1999, some of these new companies were expanding at five times the rate at which the e-business consulting practices of larger firms were expanding. A new benchmark had been set.
- *Improved profitability:* The fee-based model of consulting has always meant that the revenue of a firm has always been limited to the number of people it can attract, and its profitability by the costs of those recruits. E-business exacerbated this problem, as consultancies found themselves looking enviously at the much higher rates of return being earned by software companies whose products, once developed, could be mass-produced and distributed with minimal costs. The grass on the other side of the fence was definitely looking greener.
- *Defence:* Alongside the e-consulting specialists, there were numerous examples of established corporations looking to leverage their core competencies by creating spin-off consulting firms – a trend replicated by dot.coms as investors increased their pressure on them to break even. With barriers coming down between so many sectors, it seemed entirely reasonable for consulting firms to retaliate by establishing footholds in other markets.

As with other areas of the economy, the years since 1999 have seen an explosion in the number and type of alliances being forged by consulting firms. Looking at the underlying trends, four strategies have emerged:

- Vertical integration – the financial performance of the software industry continues to be highly attractive to consulting firms; concerned not to miss out on the levels of growth enjoyed by companies like SAP in the 1990s, consulting firms have been taking equity stakes in the companies they believe will grow rapidly in the future.

- Value chain integration – a minority of consulting firms, often the more strategically-focused ones – have tried to position themselves as prime contractors, capable of pulling together the disparate groups of highly specialised consultants required by complex e-business projects.
- Aggregation – an even smaller number of the largest firms experimented with using their collective assets and/or client contacts to give them economic muscle in new markets (Chapter 1 cites the example of PwC's E-conomy, aimed at passing on the bulk discount PwC could negotiate on its own behalf, to small businesses).
- Becoming 'holding companies' – Chapter 1 also makes the point that consulting firms were far better positioned than most of their clients to exploit the opportunities of a e-business; the best firms, like their clients, had in-depth knowledge of specific domains, but they coupled this with a far-reaching and varied client network – the kind of network needed in order to pull together a new, cross-sector business. All that consulting firms had historically lacked, if they were to maximise this opportunity, was a willingness to focus on – ally with, in effect – a small number of sectors, rather than trying to be all things to all clients. Going beyond their traditional, facilitative role, some consulting firms looked to be establishing themselves as industry players in their own right.

The Continued Benefits of Networking

But the collapse of the dot.com market and retrenchment in the venture capital community inevitably raises serious questions over the sustainability and desirability of these strategies. The economic incentive has largely gone, as consulting firms – once again – find themselves in the highest echelons of profitability. The threat of the new entrants has receded, as these find themselves under pressure from their investors to sacrifice growth for profitability.

The e-business implosion may have taken away the economic rationale for diversification, but the four key benefits for consultancies of networking still hold good.

(1) Accessing new types of intellectual capital

In the original edition of this book, it was argued that clients of the future are likely to be far more voracious in their demands for new intellectual capital: they will not simply want more new ideas, but a steady stream of them, providing tangible assurance that they are not falling behind their competitors. This point has been reinforced by the experience of e-business: as Chapter 5 suggests, for consulting firms to avoid repetitions of the boom-bust model of 1999–2001, then that steady stream of new ideas is important for them as well as for their clients. One solution to this will be for consulting firms to manage their intellectual capital much more effectively, but firms will also have to look for partners who can provide new, complementary intellectual capital. Moreover, as client industries converge further, the intellectual capital to which they want access may well be outside the normal reach of a single consulting firm.

(2) Using instant critical mass to take control

Purchasing new intellectual capital, or acquiring it *via* alliances or mergers, will not just be important on the micro – individual client – level. Rather than taking time to develop a new service or access a new market organically, e-business has shown that acquisition provides an almost immediate *entrée* into new areas. Rather than going in unprepared, the consulting firm has been able to buy fully fledged expertise with which it can make an immediate impact. Such an impact is essential if a firm is to establish dominance of the market concerned. It used to be the case that the markets for specific consulting services emerged gradually, often over some time. Perhaps it is a management culture of increasing instant gratification; perhaps it is simply the fact that we have much better access to information than we had ten, even five, years ago: whatever the reason, we seem to live now in a world in which consulting markets are created almost instantly. The opportunity for a firm to build up its expertise is already shrinking fast: in consulting parlance 'you have to hit the ground running'. Being able to play the leading role in these markets – rather than simply have a bit part – will be crucial, if only to justify the level of investment required to enter it. And having a leading role will be dependent on getting on stage first. Forging alliances which provide instant new services will be the key way in which a consulting firm can be first to market, and can then use its pre-eminent position to control the development of the market. Alliances, in effect, will give consulting firms the chance to create, not just new services, but entire new markets.

(3) Creating greater differentiation

Most consulting firms – large and small firms alike – are bad at making choices. This stems partly from a desire to remain genuinely responsive to client needs (clients therefore decide for consultants what the latter's future services and markets will be), and partly from having inclusive decision-making processes which, while strong at creating consensus, are weak when it comes to making difficult choices. For this reason, many of the alliances formed in the consulting industry in the past have been the products of opportunist instinct rather than a well-honed strategy. The result of this – and this is something that we will be exploring in greater depth in the following chapter – is that most consulting firms have failed to differentiate themselves.

Creating alliances represents a partial solution to this so far intractable problem. Consulting firms are just starting to wake up to the idea that there are only a finite number of possible combinations or networks. Make the wrong choice now and you could see yourself excluded from lucrative markets in the future. Make the right choice and you will have created a powerful barrier to entry. In effect, alliances provide an important opportunity for resolving the branding and differentiation issues which haunt the industry at the moment.

But with only a certain number of alliances to develop – like land to carve up – it is clear that consulting firms will need to make much clearer, more consistent choices than they have in the past. If you end up with 50 alliances, but spread across as many sectors or services, then your efforts will have been wasted. Consultancies, therefore, will need to choose the ground for which they wish to stake a claim: will they ally with a company that offers synergistic services into established markets, or will they link up with someone who can give them access to a new market?

(4) Protecting oneself

It's likely that alliances will continue to play a defensive role. We have already discussed how being able to access and own intellectual capital reserves will be one of the key determining factors of success over the next few years. But asserting ownership and litigation represent only one way for a consulting firm to establish and defend its intellectual assets. *De facto* control can be achieved where a firm is prepared to create alliances between itself, the originators of the intellectual capital (or parts of it) and the consumers of it (clients) – in effect, vertical integration of the intellectual capital value chain.

But these benefits apply almost wholly to the 'core' consulting market: does the collapse of the first wave of e-businesses also mark the end of an experiment in which consulting firms looked to diversify beyond the conventional confines of their industry? Will consulting firms return to their traditional role, or will the changes of the last two years have a long-term impact on the industry?

The Last Source of Competitive Advantage?

The one overriding reason why consulting firms are likely to continue their forays into other sectors – albeit on a more low-key basis than those they made at the height of the initial e-business boom – is that it *may* – and I stress may – offer a source of competitive advantage.

Of all the Holy Grails in business, competitive advantage in consulting has to be one of the most difficult to find. And worse, just when you think you've got it in your hands, it evaporates, as one of your competitors copies your approach. I am always amazed by how often I hear the same things from different firms. In 1999, when the talk was that the basic economic rules were changing, even the newest of the new firms were still talking about adding 'value' to clients and 'working in partnership' with them, as if the significance of these terms hadn't been diminished by being used (and abused) by just about every single incumbent player, and as if these terms could somehow differentiate them. What became clear was just how irresistible the language of consultancy is: however different they wanted to sound, these firms still wanted to sound like consultants. 'Most of the major [consulting] players are working to very similar formulas', concluded a study of the industry in the *Financial Times*. 'They have grown at broadly uniform rates in recent years on the back of a surging market. Aside from the impact of mergers and acquisitions – motivated by economies of scale and scope – relative competitive positions have remained fairly constant, despite much rhetoric to the contrary.'[2]

When you come to consider it, it seems extraordinary that an industry that is so intangible, so intellectual rather than physical, finds it so hard to change, to do something differently.

Let's try an experiment. Look at a ball-bearing manufacturer: what are its options for creating competitive advantage in a mature, highly standardised, essentially physical business? It has two possibilities. It can strengthen its hold over the demand side of business, by improving its product (performance, availability, and so on) and/or cutting its costs, and passing at least some of the savings on as price reductions to its customers. Or it can increase its power over the supply-side, by, for example, exerting control over its raw materials by integrating with its suppliers.

Now let's look at a consulting firm. It has the same two options, but the way in which it can approach them is, I'd suggest, significantly different. Most recent networking activity in the consulting sector has been on the supply side: consultants have sought to secure their customer base by locking themselves and their customers into specific suppliers. Most collaborative ventures have therefore focused on the exchange of intellectual capital and sales opportunities between consultants and suppliers, the objective being to reduce a client's incentive to switch supplier, rather than (as for the manufacturer) reduce costs. The same is true for demand-side collaboration, where it exists: its purpose is not so much to improve the quality of the service provided – although this may be a fortuitous by-product – but to lock customers in.

If we cast our minds back to the thinking behind Brian Arthur's Law of Increasing Returns (see Chapter 5), there are three factors that distinguish organisations that enjoy increasing returns: high up-front investment (which keeps out competitors); minimal costs of production and distribution (meaning that the organisation can grow without its cost-base rising significantly); and 'customer lock-in' (whereby a proprietary methodology or technical standard becomes a significant barrier to switching suppliers). Unwilling to do the first of these, and unable to do the second, consulting firms are concentrating on the third as critical to their future success. Thus, the focus of collaboration within the consulting industry is already beginning to shift, to encompass customers as well as suppliers, and to position the consulting firm as the crucial broker between the two. Consulting firms are playing crucial roles in bringing together groups of clients, in creating eco-systems of multiple players rather than solving the problems of them each independently. And they're reinforcing this role by taking a financial stake in the partnerships they create, in which they are rapidly becoming equal players. Furthermore, pursuing this strategy may also give consultancies access to the two other components of 'increasing returns'. Often these partnerships do require the level of up-front commitment, either in cash or time, which firms have – when left to their own devices – been unwilling to sanction. Equally, in order to be clear what the value is that they bring (and pure partnership facilitation will always be difficult to value in isolation), consulting firms are often taking roles which take them beyond consultancy, notably into software development.

It is therefore in these client collaborations that consulting firms may find the differentiation and competitive advantage that have traditionally eluded them. It's a strategy that's not without risks: as someone on Star Trek might have put it, 'it's consulting – but not as we know it'.

---

1 Benjamin Gomes-Casseres, *The Alliance Revolution: The New Shape of Business Rivalry* (Cambridge, MA: Harvard, 1997), p. 2.

2 *Financial Times*, 2 November 1998.

7

The Right People: Specialisation and Beyond

E-business may have changed much of the consulting industry, but some things remain the same: the importance of people, and the difficulty of finding (and keeping) the right balance of skills. Or do they? Does the networking environment of the future, and the changing role that consultants will play within it, mean that the industry needs a different kind of person?

Generalisation *versus* Specialisation

Consultancy has always been a balance between generalisation and specialisation. Even in the smallest, most focused firms, the specialist consultant has been expected to complement his or her specific skills with a broad understanding of the business environment as a whole. Indeed, it is often this combination that has been used to distinguish 'consultants' from that lower breed of outsider, the 'contractor'. Somewhere along the line, the ideal of the 'T-shaped' consultant was born: someone who was capable of generalist knowledge across a wide range of areas, complemented by an in-depth understanding of one specific area.

The arguments for specialisation and generalisation are like those for outsourcing *versus* insourcing: fashion seems to swing in favour of one and then the other; the death of one is announced only for it to be suddenly resurrected the following year. Will this oscillation continue in the future, or should we expect to see a decisive move towards one approach?

To be able to answer this question, we first need to examine the drivers for and against each approach.

On the generalist side, the main factors have been: credibility and the need, first, for flexibility and second, cohesion. Taking credibility first: the ability to think broadly has not just been a distinguishing feature between a consultant and a contractor. It has also been a means by which consultants ensure that they are perceived to be – at least – their clients' equal (specialisation being the consultant's advantage over the client). It is the consultancy equivalent of general management. Just as a client company will put its most valuable staff through a career development programme which is designed to give them the necessary skills and breadth of exposure to allow them to progress to senior management positions, so a consultancy needs to ensure that its consultants can hold their own at board level by demonstrating comparable credentials. The importance of generalisation in consultancy is therefore directly correlated with the perceived importance of the concept of 'general management' to business.

But, if generalisation is important in terms of credibility, it is considerably more important internally. Ensuring that its consultants have some degree of general business understanding gives a consulting firm the flexibility to identify opportunities for new business, to change focus where a specific skill becomes redundant and – conversely – to move resources to areas of high demand. Put at its simplest, generalisation creates flexibility, and flexibility creates profits.

Furthermore, flexibility provides a degree of cohesion. There is relatively little 'glue' holding consultancy organisations together: few firms are held together by strong brands, established products or – even – long-standing client relationships. Staff turnover among consultants may be as high as 30 per cent, but, even over the course of the average 3–4 year stint with a particular firm, much of a consultant's time will be spent out on clients' sites. Specialisation leads to organisational fragmentation, and generalisation is one of the few offsetting factors that consulting firms have at their disposal. Giving up their generalist characteristics could also endanger their ability to get people to work together.

This raises the important issue of synergy. Are consulting firms synergistic? What can the 'mega-firms' do that small consultants cannot? In the consulting industry – unlike, say, manufacturing – synergies do not necessarily give rise to economies of scale – as evidenced by the fact that the fee rates for small consultancies are often much lower. The advantages of size lie in the level of investment possible, global reach, flexibility of resources and the ability to address client issues from multiple directions. But all these advantages become much more difficult to realise without generalisation. Generalisation, therefore, is the essential channel for synergy: without it, the different parts of consulting organisations would not be able to talk to each other, let alone work together.

What then are the factors that push consulting firms in the opposite direction – towards specialisation? By contrast with generalisation – which is fundamentally driven by internal needs – the pressure for specialisation comes from external sources: the need to be able to deliver added value services and to demonstrate a differentiated positioning in the marketplace. Specialisation is one of the primary means by which consulting firms distinguish themselves from their competitors (a point which was covered in greater depth in the previous chapter).

In a market in which management theories often look homogeneous and innovative ideas can be copied almost instantly, depth – rather than breadth – of experience has become essential in clients' eyes. Being able to field, not just a national expert, but an international expert in a specific area is already a critical success factor in winning some types of new business. This pressure from clients is fuelled by several factors: the declining role of the general business manager, the increased complexity of almost all areas of management which means that functional directors have to be experts as much as co-ordinators, and perhaps a growing cynicism about management theory. In a world where the value of an intangible service is a hotly debated topic, being able to demonstrate specialist know-how is tantamount to proving your worth. There are few clients who would be prepared to pay a lot of money for a generalist, however good: there are many who already are paying a great deal for specialists with particularly in-depth understanding of an area of specific relevance. Part of the reason for this is obvious – a specialist has the skills the client organisation lacks – but other parts are more subtle. Clients perceive specialists as able to provide a solution that generalists – clients themselves, in effect – cannot provide for themselves. Having a specialist skill implies a special solution. Buying specialists also puts the client in control: it is the client who has defined the problem and identified the kind of expertise required to resolve it. By contrast, generalist consultants have a greater opportunity to set the agenda.

If anything, e-business reinforced – indeed, strengthened – this message. Specialisation became fundamentally associated, in clients' eyes, with credibility: in a market full of instant experts, in-depth knowledge became the hallmark of a valuable consultant. As a result, the key problem mentioned then – the need to marry specialisation with flexibility – remains as pertinent today as it was two years ago.

Flexibility is essential to the consulting industry. It allows firms to move resources from declining to expanding markets with minimal upheaval. It means that the skills and intellectual capital it has amassed in one sector can be redeployed in another. How will consulting firms cope with the reduced flexibility that accompanies specialisation?

The first step will be to recognise it as a problem. At the moment, the combined generalist/specialist option – that 'T-shaped' consultant – has been a means of avoiding the issue. In the absence of any structural balance between the two approaches, it has effectively been the responsibility of individual consultants (aided by the relevant training) to reconcile them. But, as that personal balance becomes harder to maintain – indeed, as there is less of an incentive to maintain it, as career development will depend on specialisation rather than general business knowledge – firms will have to take on greater corporate responsibility for finding a solution.

One approach would be to encourage consultants to be generalists up to a certain grade/seniority and to specialise thereafter – making explicit what happens in many firms implicitly. The problem, however, will be that the economic advantages of specialisation – as partners/directors try to leverage their very expensive time with specialised support – will put pressure on the organisation to start the process of becoming specialised sooner rather than later. Thus, specialisation will, over time, start at more and more junior grades: except in the most homogeneous of consulting firms and markets, the level of generalisation will be difficult to control and sustain.

The more heterogeneous firms may find it easier to employ more freelance consultants – 'free agents' as they increasingly call themselves in the US, so that flexibility is maintained through multiple short-term contracts instead of employing large numbers of people on a permanent basis. This is a model which makes particularly good sense if we accept that the turnover rates of intellectual capital are likely to increase. Rather than accepting that a consultant has a shelf life of 10–20 years, we may need to recognise that the equivalent shelf-life in the future may be less than five years and that, rather than stay with a consulting firm for a long period, a consultant needs to move in and out, recharging his/her intellectual capital either by working in industry or by formal training. Effectively, this route allows market forces to solve the problem for the consulting firms, because individuals – in order to ensure their continued employability – will adapt to changing environments much more quickly than any institutional training programme could. Rather than 'T-shaped' consultants, we will essentially have consultants who are just the stem of the 'T', but are likely to be several such 'stems' over the course of their working lives.

However, while this model makes for enormous and self-sustaining flexibility, it will not be easy to manage. If consultancies are increasingly struggling to attract the best people from what they see to be a dwindling pool of qualified resources, then surely a system in which they are having to negotiate for all of these people all of the time will leave them considerably more vulnerable to being unable to meet demand when required?

Consulting firms will need a new human resource model to be able to deal with this issue – something which few firms have even started to consider.

Theory *versus* Practice: The Growth of 'Real' Consultants

But e-business didn't just accentuate the importance of specialisation: another facet of the consultant, which is turning out to be of almost equal importance, is the extent to which he or she is a 'real' person. 'We don't just want people who'll come and spout the party line at us', said one client. 'Nor do we want people who've gathered lots of data and can talk about a subject only in theory. We want people who believe in what they're saying and who've had direct, practical experience of the kinds of issues we face.'

Acquiring new technical skills is something the consulting industry has traditionally taken in its stride, helped by firms' typically high turnover of consultants (which has brought in a constant stream of new skill sets) and their significant on-going investment in staff development (which has been able to retrain existing staff). Restructuring the consultancy workforce in the past has therefore been possible with little visible upheaval.

E-business challenged this way of doing things. As the Internet made vast quantities of information significantly easier to access, the disparity in information about business trends which has traditionally distinguished consultants from their clients was eroded: each side was using the same sources of data and had roughly equivalent levels of market information. It was therefore much easier for clients to spot consultants who didn't know their subject, whose understanding of e-business trends had perhaps come from a couple of weeks' intensive training. Moreover, clients were also looking for something more than technical know-how: 'we weren't just looking to acquire specific expertise', recalled one, 'but also to see a different kind of culture in action. It was a question of doing, as much as knowing.' Not surprisingly, the new entrants enjoyed a substantial advantage as a result of this: the 'old' economy firms were seen to be hide-bound by bureaucratic processes, whereas the new firms offered more flexible working and better skills integration: they wanted consultants who were more in tune with the entrepreneurial environment of the moment.

There was little the established firms could do. With many consultants already leaving the profession and joining dot.coms, recruitment was difficult and retraining the only viable option. In many firms, the focus of the training was on developing a wider and deeper understanding of the business issues facing clients in the new economy, even though most clients were sceptical of its value, for two reasons. First, it was perceived as continuing – indeed, reinforcing – the long-standing dichotomy of business and technology consulting skills in a market where this division is increasingly irrelevant. Second, and perhaps more importantly, such training inevitably was seen to concentrate on 'best practice' – on what leading businesses had already achieved – rather than looking forward to future sources of competitive advantage. This kind of information has long been the staple of the consulting industry, particularly in the more business/operational sectors of the market, but it, too, has become irrelevant given the speed of change in the e-business world. Essentially, they were doubtful of the value of theorising about e-business. What mattered was the ability to take ideas and apply them in practice, without the intervening stage of theorisation; this, in turn, comes down to practical experience and flexibility – neither of which can be taught.

This challenges, not just the conventional form of training within the consulting industry, but also the fundamental role of a consultant. The overwhelming majority of consulting work is predicated on the notion that it is possible to extract the lessons from one client, or from one industry, and apply them to others. This is not to imply that consultants are not creative: identifying parallels between different industries can yield highly innovative results. It does, however, make the point that consultants are accustomed to working in a known universe, where the outcomes – whether at the macro or micro-economic levels - are fairly predictable. 'Theory' is important because it highlights the underlying trends and expected behaviours.

I believe that this shift, in terms of client preferences, towards consultants as people with practical experience, rather than as purveyors of theory, is irreversible. Just because the driving momentum of e-business has disappeared, it does not mean that consultants will be able to rely on theory as they have in the past. As one client put it, 'in the past, the reputation of individual consultants was based upon their breadth and depth of knowledge. Thus, a top consultant might have had twenty years of consulting in a particular sector, but no one demanded that he or she have line management experience there. Today, hands-on experience is the number one thing we're looking for when we evaluate a consultancy. They have to have been there, and done it.' For many clients, practical experience offers a solution to many of the concerns they have had about the consulting industry in the past. One client summed up his experience thus: 'consultants with practical know-how are very different kinds of people. They tend to be much more committed to a project: the idea of doing a part of something, and then leaving someone else – whether that's the client or another consulting firm – to finish the job is a complete anathema to them. They want to see something through from start to finish.' According to another client I spoke to, this commitment to the end as well as the means had ramifications for the way in which the consultant engaged with the client organisation: 'what we've found is that these people tend to rely less on facts and figures than traditional consultants. I don't mean to suggest that their cavalier, but simply that, because they've done something before, they believe in it – and that communicates itself to the client organisation. Typical consultants would give you a detailed report, a series of options and stand back while you took the decision. A more hands-on consultant will say what he or she thinks you should do, and why. They're opinionated.' From the client perspective, consultants with practical experience are also far less concerned with following a standardised methodology and are more willing to take on risks, rather than refer decisions up a chain of command. One person I spoke to put it this way: 'The front-line consultants working in client organisations are having to make more important decisions than would have been the case ten, or even five, years ago. The senior partner can't always know what's going on: he or she has to rely on enrolling people behind common goals, rather than to manage risk on a systematic basis.' 'Survival', as another person put it, 'will depend on good judgement and self-confidence, just as much more as it will depend on technical know-how'.

From the consulting perspective, practical experience has also gone hand-in-hand with much greater flexibility. One consultant I interviewed recalled a project where the client had a great new idea half way through: 'we'd just completed 50 per cent of the work and, suddenly, everything had to change. You have to have people that can cope with that type of situation, who won't feel crushed to have throw away so much work in which they'd already invested a lot of effort.'

Key to the future will be empowerment, liberating consultants from the processes and chains of command, allowing them to work on an equal basis with people with other skill-sets while encouraging them to deepen the specialist expertise which will engender respect internally and externally. But empowered and flexible consultants still need back-up. Having a strong sense of identify distinguishes the new e-consulting companies at the corporate level, but it's also significant that this attitude flows through their organisations: you can only give a consultant responsibility if you believe in them: 'we have to support our staff 100 per cent of the time', said a chief executive of one consulting firm, 'even where we know that what we're saying to the client isn't always welcome. It's something that's fundamental to our culture.'

Many consulting firms have yet to recognise the extent of change facing them, if they're to adapt to the era of the 'real' consultant. As one partner put it: 'conventional consulting has been a highly successful, profitable business model and a lot of firms are simply making too much money. In some cases, it'll take a major catastrophe before they can even begin to countenance the level of change required. The type of leadership, the decision-making processes, the line management will all need to change if they're to respond effectively to the needs of e-business clients.' 'Most consulting firms aren't in a position to *do* things', commented another, 'their strength has lain in thinking about business issues – rather than in software or hardware development'.

Some firms – a tiny minority – are taking a more innovative approach, and are using their organisational structure to create the combination of in-depth, specialist knowledge and hands-on experience in the real world which clients are most eager to obtain. One such is Bain & Co (see Case Study 7.1).

confident knowledge that that experience will, in turn, prove invaluable once they come back into the main consulting firm.' According to Gerry Mulvin, Bain considered making bainlab completely separate in organisational, as well as legal, terms: 'but that just didn't feel right to us. We wanted a model in which we could develop and integrate people's skills, not create divisions between them. We also wanted to provide the type of learning environment which would attract – and reattract – the best people to us, but without necessarily assuming that everyone would want to stay with us for the duration of their careers.'

The key to the future – and I suspect that Bain gives us a taste of this – will lie in finding creative ways of reconciling apparently irreconcilable issues: integrating multiple specialist skills without losing the focus of any one; balancing individual heterogeneity with corporate homogeneity; combining theory and practice.

8

New Organisational Models

In Chapters 5 and 6, I discussed the increasing interconnectivity of the industry, both in terms of links between consulting firms, and between consulting firms and their clients. In Chapter 7, I looked at the ramifications this has at the level of individual consultants, in terms of the kinds of skills and mindset required. But all of these points have implications for the structure of the consulting organisation.

Consultancy – A People Business

Before trying to analyse these implications, it's important to reiterate some of the points about the consulting industry's dependency on people.

Many organisations pay lip service to the idea of being a 'people business', but it remains hard to conceive of an industry which is more genuinely dependent on its people than consultancy. The core consulting process has involved experienced individuals reapplying their skills in new situations, thinking on their feet, and working closely with their clients' people. And it has been heresy – until very recently – to suggest that it could, or should, be otherwise. People have been the source of fundamental strength to the consulting industry, translating what could so easily be – and often is – seen as irrelevant management theory into concepts and working practices that clients initially understand and ultimately value. You only have to scan the annual reports and promotional material prepared by consultancies to see how important the people factor is: intangible services are made concrete by including pictures and thumbnail sketches of the consultants involved.

While the consulting labour market may have eased somewhat in late 2000, as the first influx of people from failed dot.coms made their presence felt, recruitment remains high on the list of any firm's priorities. These days, however, it's quality, not quantity, that's key.

That being said, the solutions remain the same. Firms are changing their recruitment profile, either in order to recruit older and much more experienced people, or to attract people from very different backgrounds (astrophysicists rather than business school graduates). They are also taking into account the shift in attitudes among a younger generation of recruits, people who may be looking for a more balanced lifestyle, rather than the ambitious and dedicated recruits who characterised the 1980s. To accommodate this preference for more flexible working, they're changing their own organisational structures: job-sharing, a greater number of freelance consultants, and so on. The relationship between the firm and these 'semi-detached' employees may be quite different, with individuals not only taking responsibility for their own career development but funding it as well, as consultancies become less and less prepared to invest in training where they know that the recipient is likely to leave in less than five years. Consultancies will still provide training – indeed, one can foresee that they will provide more and more as the educational system fails to deliver recruits of the level required – but it may be that it is the individual consultant who pays for it, motivated by the need to keep his/her individual CV up to date.

But, whatever the solution tried, attracting and retaining people more effectively is unlikely to be the complete solution. Perhaps there is a single, perfect solution that, when it is found, will genuinely create a sustainable competitive advantage for the winning firm, that one firm will find a strategy which means that its rivals become chronically – fatally – under-resourced. However, it seems more likely that such changes, as they are made, will be mimicked by competitors. Changes in the culture and management of firms take time to have an impact – time enough for other firms to catch up. Changing the way consultants manage their people asset is unlikely to be enough to solve the underlying problem of scarce resources.

Moreover, none of this changes the fact that economies of scale have been notoriously difficult to achieve within the consulting industry. People may enable growth, but they can also be an obstacle towards greater profitability. Profitability across the industry is determined, not just by the extent to which consultants are 'utilised' and their individual fee rates, but by the ratio of staff to partners or directors. But, irrespective of the relative profitability of firms across the industry as a whole, the fact that time and materials tend to be by far the dominant source of income means that the extent to which an individual firm can improve its profitability is limited. Unlike a software firm, for example, a consultancy cannot obviously develop something and then produce it at virtually no extra cost. Unlike merchant banks, consultants have not charged premium sums for passing on information about, say, an opportunity to a potentially interested party. Consultancies can – and do – put up their daily rates, but their profitability is still restricted by the number of hours their staff can work. In an environment where companies – particularly high-tech companies – are earning higher margins by exploiting their intellectual capital in different ways, it cannot be long before consulting firms start to look actively at alternative methods of generating profits. Just because the operational model they have had has worked to date, does not mean that it is going to be a sufficiently effective model going forward.

The Impact of Technology

American academic James Brian Quinn has argued that new technologies 'tend to invade and diffuse through service industries in more or less predictable ways', by initiating sequential economic changes and creating new strategic opportunities.[1]

- New *economies of scale* are the first to appear, and result in the centralisation of key service activities into large institutions, with many smaller enterprises which lack capital and expertise being driven out. Subsequently, renewed decentralisation occurs as smaller units in more dispersed locations link into networks to provide feeder operations for the larger enterprises.
- A powerful second order effect comes in terms of new *economies of scope*, as the new technologies allow service enterprises to handle a much wider array of data, output functions or customers without significant cost increases.
- As the new technologies begin to be used more effectively, organisations find themselves better able to cope with *increased complexity*.
- *Disintermediation* is often a consequence of this process. Given a company's large scale and technological power, outside parties seek to connect to the company that is innovating in the system rather than go through intermediaries.
- *Deregulation* becomes a viable policy option in many areas as extensive cross-competition becomes possible.

- Finally, *redispersion and redecentralisation* occur, as centralisation and disintermediation create a counter-need for more localisation and personalised contact in each of the service areas. Thus, the technology achieves a new level of outreach and connectivity to the marketplace, and many new enterprises appear in emerging small niches. Usually the customer is the beneficiary.

To what extent have – or are – these changes having an effect on the organisational models that underpin the consulting industry?

Economies of scale and scope: increased complexity

I think there's no question about it: effective knowledge management is critical, if consulting firms are to create any economies of scale and scope, and prove themselves capable of handling a much more diverse and highly specialised base of clients and consultants. As one commentator recently concluded:

> Knowledge management is perhaps the most critical process within the firm. It is certainly the case for the consulting industry, where the firm's core product is knowledge itself. Consultants live and breathe knowledge management because they sell business solutions and knowledge itself. Producing and selling knowledge constitutes their core resource or asset. Knowledge management is the basic 'production technology' their consultants rely upon and, with recent changes in the computer industry, this technology is undergoing a revolution.[2]

Despite the centrality of knowledge to the consulting process, the consulting industry has, in general, been slow to manage its knowledge assets on a systematic basis. Knowledge management has been a reactive activity in which the consultant, responding to a request from a client, pulls together the firm's knowledge in a specific area. The Internet and web-based technologies have not materially changed this, but they have allowed firms to gather more disparate sets of information more quickly than ever before, and make them more accessible. 'Our original knowledge management network was quite hard to use', recalled one partner I talked to, 'but the new technologies have given us an opportunity to develop a much more accessible system in which we can use search engines to pinpoint the knowledge we really want.' Some firms are also trying to make better use of their internal data, using web-technology to streamline internal processes and supplier interfaces. Some are going as far as introducing internal exchanges for resources which enable managers to bid for resources. Being able to set daily internal prices and run auctions may soon follow.

While all of these developments promise some degree of greater internal efficiency, they don't offer a paradigm shift. To do the latter, consulting firms will have to take a more proactive, less opportunistic approach to gathering, analysing and valuing their knowledge. This will be a matter of survival: clients have too many other sources of information to be interested in anything other than in-depth analysis (as investment banks are finding to their cost) – and in-depth analysis cannot be created instantly, but requires long-term investment and dedicated resources.

But as Quinn's model suggests, economies of scale and scope both involve an increased level of centralisation: using knowledge management as the prime means of achieving these economies will inevitably mean that the knowledge contained within them, and the uses to which the knowledge is put, become more standardised. Improved knowledge management therefore tends to go with either greater uniformity of delivery or an increased focus on a specific sector. One strategy, for example, is to focus on those service areas (notably in IT-related consultancy) where it has been possible to develop a standardised approach. IT assignments provide a regular source of income which can be used on training and development, and investing in new products. And, because IT-related work is a more homogeneous market than traditional consulting markets, it is easier to develop standard training courses and methodologies that reduce the need to recruit specialised people and minimise the risk of problems. As a result, the ratio of partners to staff is much lower than for less IT-orientated firms. An alternative approach has been to specialise in a small number of areas which precludes the need to build up diverse knowledge assets across the board.

However, a more serious problem with knowledge management lies in the extent to which it not only permits, but may even encourage, the deskilling of the consulting industry. Several clients I interviewed recalled being sent proposals by consulting firms which were largely drawn from their knowledge of management systems. 'The range of information was stunning', said one, 'it was a genuinely impressive survey of similar projects in other organisations. The problem lay in the people who came to present their approach: it was clear that none of them had been involved in any of the engagements discussed. They may have been fine consultants, but in comparison to our expectations, they came over as completely inexperienced and lacking in depth.'

Moreover, knowledge, once standardised, is more likely to be converted into software, and thus the consulting industry stands in danger of cannibalising its own products. When a consulting firm develops some new knowledge – a way to optimise R&D expenditure, for example – it does so with the aim of increasing sales. If the service proves very successful it may find itself with too many clients and not enough consultants to do the work (one of the classic limitations of the people model in practice). To overcome this, it may convert part or all of that intellectual capital into a software package (in this case, perhaps a computer model which carries out the actual process of optimisation). Doing so will allow the firm to earn higher than normal profits, because it will be able to carry out more 'consultancy' with fewer people. But higher profits will, in turn, attract other players, notably software houses which would then develop their own 'packaged' version of this service. By incorporating the new application into their existing software (as a special module, say) the software company will be able to tap into an existing client base much more readily than the consulting firm: if an organisation already has the software company's financial package, they will probably be interested in a new module which will both reduce their R&D budgets and can be easily and cost-effectively integrated with their existing systems. Coming from the software company, which will not be burdened with the development costs of having to think up the idea in the first place, the software package will also be cheaper. In the battle between the two, the software house will probably be the victor: clients will continue to buy the idea, but not from the consulting firm – which is, effectively, back to square one.

Providing the consulting firm can continue to generate new intellectual capital, this scenario will not prove disastrous, but once the speed with which those ideas can be generated falls behind the time it takes to convert them into software packages, consulting firms will be facing a market in which their ideas are cannibalised, almost before they have taken them out to clients.

It is probably an inevitable development – in fact we can already see signs of it in some very specialised areas of consulting. For example, some types of tax review, which only a couple of years ago would have been done by a team of tax specialists, can now be done much more effectively by computer models. Computerised benchmarking tools are also only automating what until recently would have been conventional consulting assignments. If the situation is here to stay, then the imperative for consultancies will be to try to take control of the process, to initiate and manage the conversion of their ideas into software by allying themselves closely with software houses, even acquiring their own software houses. It seems inevitable, therefore, that the distinction that largely exists at present between consultancy and software will start to blur significantly.

Reintermediation

In Chapter 5, I touched upon the notion that the consulting firm itself could be regarded as a classic intermediary, and one which may be disintermediated. But the fragmentation of the consulting market and the diversity of client needs means that, at least in the short term, the 'centre' is likely to have some role to play.

Certainly where the traditional partnership structure is concerned, the corporate entity that constitutes the firm has typically been driven by coalitions between these business units, rather than by any push from the centre. If the centre is to add value, then it comes, first, from helping the local practice perform its function more effectively and, second, from targeting those clients which may be beyond the reach of any one local practice (such as multinational clients). Indeed, this message has been reinforced since 1999, by the advantage clearly enjoyed by many of the new entrants who were unencumbered by the dispersed management structure of a partnership, and, as a result, found themselves more able to direct their resources and people in a more focused way.

It's important to recognise here that increased specialisation (discussed in Chapter 7) will have a significant impact on the organisation as a whole, as well as the individuals within it. In the first place, as the specialist areas become more clearly defined – 'deeper', if you like – and the divide between specialisms greater, it is inevitable that different agendas will start to emerge. It will also become harder to identify a common strategy which is more than the sum of its individual parts. Second, and as a direct result of these divergent strategies, the value the centre is able to add gets less: looking at the world from a centralist, generalist perspective will not help these individual business units. Even centralised functions, such as training and career development, may be much less relevant, as each specialist area will have its own needs. Much more helpful to the specialist business unit – and this is the third and most important effect of specialisation as a whole – will be to be able to link up to its parallel units in other parts of the world. In other words, the extent of integration by specialism within global consulting organisations will be much greater than at present, where the national firm structure often tends to come between the local specialist group and their counterparts elsewhere. Thus, the specialist team dealing with, for example, supply chain management, will forge links with other supply chain management teams.

Being reliant on people and intellectual capital, consulting firms are fluid, self-adapting organisations. As it becomes clear that the greatest value to be added comes from the closer collaboration of groups of people across the world who are working in the same specialised field, the structure of the firms will adapt to accommodate this. Thus, the role of the national, even that of the international firm, becomes subsumed into the specialist structure. Clearly, in practice, this may apply to some specialisms more than others, but, overall, we should expect to see this kind of model emerge.

As a model, it obviously poses a serious threat to the one-firm concept: inter-specialism networking is both harder to achieve and – from the point of view of the specialists themselves – increasingly irrelevant; the specialist sub-brands may start to compete with a firm's overall brand. Most significantly, it may change the rules of competition within the industry. As we discussed in the previous chapter, competition between consulting firms occurs on many fronts, largely because the distinctions – at least between the major firms – are slight. By contrast, niche players have a tremendous advantage because they can develop clear – specialist – reputations in their chosen markets. As the specialisms within generalist firms emerge much more strongly, there will be fewer points of overlap and the level of direct competition will decline. This changing competitive landscape begs a further question: to what extent will the collaboration between specialist areas go beyond the boundaries of single firms? After all, it follows that if the greatest synergy within a firm will be between similar, but geographically dispersed specialisms, why should this synergy stop at the gates?

This will undoubtedly be a thin-end-of-the-wedge issue. As clients' demands become more precise and the level of specialisation deeper, individual business units will start to look for additional skills. Some of them will find what they need through organic staff development or recruitment, but others will create links with similar groups of specialists elsewhere. The number of firms operating in each specialist market will decrease: competition will be between groups of related specialists, rather than between individual firms. Over time, we may even see quasi-monopolies emerging in some areas, especially where the specialism itself is new and resources comparatively scarce. In order to make an impact on the market, and to meet demand they stimulate, the specialist groups from different firms, together with complementary niche players, may well have to work together. From a profitability point of view, this is unlikely to be a problem: it may even be a more profitable structure than the one we have today. But it clearly makes it more difficult to hold a multi-disciplinary firm together. With 'value' travelling up and down the specialist groupings, not across them, the glue that keeps such firms together is necessarily weaker.

What, then, will be the role of the centre? Will there be a role? Or will consulting firms simply switch to this much more vertically differentiated, even fragmented structure? Insofar as the centre does have a role, it will be in managing the risks of structures like the one envisaged here.

An area where the input of the centre will be crucial will be in the management of the portfolio. Most multi-disciplinary firms subscribe to the idea of portfolio management, although very few have made it work in reality. But it seems likely that the managing partners of the future will have to take a much more proactive role in deciding in which specialisms to invest. The generalist core of consulting firms will become much more like a holding company, whose function is to maximise the overall value of the asset for its stakeholders in acquiring, developing and disposing of specialist areas. The holding company provides a useful analogy: it will become less important to employ practising consultants in the centre, both because the role of the centre will be closer to investment management than consultancy and because, as a generation of specialists grows up, it will become increasingly difficult to find individuals with the breadth of experience to manage the service portfolio in its entirety. It also follows that, if you no longer need consultants to run a consultancy, anyone can – and probably will – start doing it. It will be logical, in the future (and once various regulatory issues have been resolved), to find investment banks and other asset management companies running, not so much consulting firms, but groups of consulting services, operating in parallel under some sort of corporate brand. We should expect to see non-consulting companies with strong existing brands exploiting those brands by offering consulting services. This has already happened to a degree within the hardware and software markets (IBM, for example, has a consulting practice which is able to exploit its parent's brand). But how long will it be before we have Coca-Cola or Virgin Consulting?

Change, however, is likely to be slight and incremental, as one specialism after another gradually establishes stronger vertical, rather than horizontal, links. It does not, therefore, spell the sudden end of the multi-disciplinary firm, although it certainly makes the latter's role a more challenging one. Instead, what we should expect to see is that the managing teams from such firms take on a more detached, holding company-style role. While other asset management companies might be looking to enter the consulting market, consulting companies – having acquired a taste for asset management – may well find themselves taking on non-consulting assets.

Redispersion

But how long will the centralised model of consulting survive?

Size in a consulting firm is an advantage or disadvantage, depending on who you talk to – at least among consultants. Small firms believe that their focus generates better value for clients; large firms believe that their range of services is what matters. But when you talk to clients, it's clear that for the majority of them size just isn't an issue. In fact, certainly on the technology side, one of the effects of e-business seems to have been to destroy the belief in monolithic suppliers (and the consultants who implement their systems). 'One thing we don't want', said one client, 'is to go back to the situation we had in the mid-1990s, when we were all spending huge amounts of money installing massive systems. We're now much more interested in tactical approaches; small packages which we adapt to rather than customise; and smaller, specialist implementation firms who won't burden us with a management overhead we no longer wish to pay.'

Consultancies used to working on a small number of very large projects will have difficulty sustaining their business model, as this 'just do it' attitude starts to permeate even large-scale, back-office engagements. A key part to the transition that these firms will have to make – and this is where many of the specialists enjoy an advantage – will be to a less-procedurally driven environment in which individual consultants take far more direct responsibility for their contribution to engagements and client success.

It's not only horizontal divisions between different organisational strata that need to go. Fundamental to the ability of consulting firms to be able to offer the multidisciplinary approach required and desired by clients, is the lowering of the internal boundaries that have conventionally separated strategists from marketeers, and both of these from technologists. Increasingly, firms are experimenting with the idea of virtual communities, in which consultants decided the areas in which they want to work and where management is less explicit, occurring more through peer pressure between the different communities, than via a conventional hierarchy. According to one such firm: 'each skills group is responsible for ensuring the quality and creativity of its thinking: that's a key way in which we're trying to ensure that specialists remain specialists. But we also make sure that each of these three competencies is represented in internal meetings and on client teams. We believe that the only way to create and maintain a genuinely multi-disciplinary environment is to ensure that no group or individual becomes too arrogant. We encourage employees to have a different sense of what it takes to make up an organisation – to understand that they're contributing to a community rather than competing for space in a hierarchy. We expect people to put client work first but, beyond that, they've the freedom to explore the multiple communities that make up our firm: we're a self-organising system.'

The word most commonly used is 'fusing' – fusing strategic, technical and creative people, rather than trying to train the same person to have all three skills. 'The stress', said one managing partner, 'is on building teams that integrate these three skills. We try and maintain balanced engagement teams, but we also try to create a positive environment in which everyone – whatever their background – feels equally valued.'

---

1 James Brian Quinn, *Intelligent Enterprise* (New York: Free Press, 1992), p. 23.

2 *California Management Review*, Winter 1999.

9

We're All Consultants Now

Consultants and clients used to think they were different. Clients used to have an asset base rooted in the physical world – plants, machinery, tangible products. By contrast, the assets of consulting firms were primarily intellectual – ideas, management practice, benchmarks from other sectors. But the last twenty years have seen a gradual shift in both camps: clients have begun to appreciate that their intellectual assets (knowledge of a world-class process for example) may be as valuable, if not more so, than their physical assets; and consulting firms have been investing in their physical infrastructure, notably in technology. As a result, clients and consultants look much more similar (see Figure 9.1).

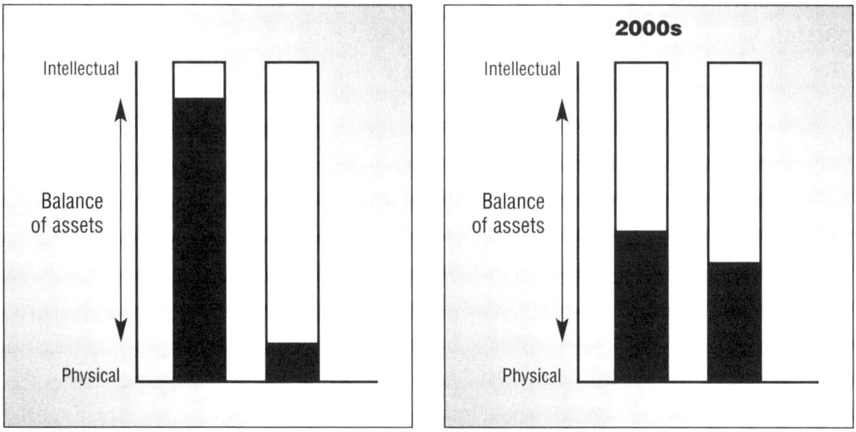

Figure 9.1 *The intellectual balance of physical and intellectual assets in consulting firms and their clients*

With the lines between them blurring, how – if at all – are consulting firms differentiating themselves? Does it matter? I'd argue that a major fault line is opening up within the consulting industry: on one side of the divide, the traditional client-consultant distinction does continue to matter; on the other, it has not only ceased to be relevant, but has even come to be seen as an impediment to future change. The two factors driving a wedge through the industry: the importance of process *versus* content; and of doing *versus* advising.

Process *versus* Content

'We don't see that we get much concrete value from a consultant coming along and facilitating processes for us: we want new ideas that we can put our fingers on', said one client. 'It's no good consultants coming in here and spouting facts: they have to have a process which helps our organisation take these facts on board and act on them', said another. It's an issue which splits clients and consulting firms down the middle.

Prior to the emergence of IT-related consultancy, the role of consultants was to provide the factual analysis which fuelled management action: most consultants were not expected to take actions themselves (something which, as we have already seen, has been an increasing source of frustration to clients). Above everything else, the industry has been characterised and defined by its facts: the bottom line for consultants was that they had more facts (in the form of wider knowledge, experience, and so on) than their clients. But, in the past 20 years, the pendulum has swung much more towards action. Facts have been less important: what has mattered has been the extent to which a group of consultants can work with a team from the client's own staff in order to help make decisions and then execute them.

All consulting assignments vary in the extent to which they involve the client. On one side of the scale, we have what we could term 'fact-based' consultancy, where the consultant is effectively hired to tell the client what to do. By contrast, 'action-based' consultancy is much more process-orientated. In this case, the means by which the ends are arrived at are as important as the ends themselves; rather than wanting to be told what to do, clients in this type of assignment want to lcarn how to decide what to do for themselves. At its most extreme form, the consulting process shifts into a secondment in which the consultant works for the client, as part of the client's own team.

The fact-based assignment model is essentially where a team of consultants is commissioned by a client to examine a particular problem and where, in resolving it, the consultants mainly rely on gathering data on the problem, analysing that data in relative isolation from the client and on a highly objective basis. To this extent, the fact-based model was the original form of consulting – this was very much the approach adopted by Frederick Taylor and the other proponents of the scientific school of management – and it continues to be a very common method of operating today. Some firms only offer this type of consulting and have constructed their differentiated brand around this style of working.

Fact-based consulting is used to resolve problems (or parts of the problem) that are:

- Discrete – that is, it is possible to use data to understand the issues involved, something which might not be possible if the problem was particularly complex and open to a variety of ill-defined variables;
- Strategic or logistical – because the analytic model relies on data, rather than softer issues such as the behaviour of people or the effectiveness of organisations, it tends to be used to address areas where data is both available and an accepted means of investigating the environment (market sizes, customer penetration levels, allocation of resources, optimal location of distribution channels, and so on); and
- Finite – an analytic approach provides a snapshot of a particular situation, but it is less effective at addressing ongoing issues where the circumstances change almost daily.

However, the crucial factor in using the fact-based consulting model is that the problem is one to which either there is a factual answer or where factual analysis will form the basis of the decision-making process. For example, a company considering moving into a new market will want – usually – to base their decision on the available facts: the size of that market, its price sensitivity, the costs of distribution, and so on. When they commission a consulting firm to undertake this analysis, they are looking to the consultants to confirm or reject the company's proposed approach. Clearly, this situation can sometimes be complicated by internal politics, but essentially it remains a question of fact: first, because it is possible to produce a factual answer to the issue (the precise detail of the answer may be limited, perhaps because of poor data, but the client will still pay attention to the findings); secondly, facts provide an acceptable basis on which the client can make its decision – that is, facts are seen to provide a reasonable justification for the venture whereas gut-feel does not.

This reliance on facts will vary from company to company, and is more a function of culture and management style: some are prepared to take decisions based on instinct which others would spend months and millions of dollars evaluating. Thus, the exact nature of the problems consultancies are asked to analyse varies widely.

However, the strength of this very analytical approach – its objectivity – is also its weakness. In the first place, the data-gathering and subsequent analysis often ignores information which is not easy to assimilate – in other words, there is often a risk in analytical assignments that the data which is gathered to fit an initial hypothesis can only ever prove or disprove that hypothesis and not suggest more lateral solutions. Secondly, almost all business situations are, in practice, open and complex: an analytical approach can only handle such complexity by essentially ignoring or simplifying it (thus, even a very well-prepared market valuation may prove wrong in practice). Thirdly – and most importantly – facts may not always be enough to change things in an organisation. It is possible for a consultant to write an excellent report, highlighting a clear action plan based on an objective assessment of the facts involved, but for his or her report never to be implemented, because either the facts used were not sufficient to galvanise the client's organisation or the client's organisation was motivated by other factors – the subjective vision of a small number of senior executives, for example – rather than objective data.

Action-based consulting has, in effect, been the industry's response to these issues. Over the past 20 years, the emphasis has been on process consulting, to the extent that even strategy firms have been forced to incorporate some aspects of implementation – 'doing' – into their work. As the name suggests, the emphasis in process consulting falls on the process by which the consulting is done, as much as on its output, the premise being that a client's organisation should be consulted 'with' rather than be presented with a *fait accompli*, as is usually the case with analytical consulting.

In a process-based assignment consultants will work with members of the client's staff to discuss, investigate and design solutions to the problems at hand: this can range from working very closely with a small number of individuals, to having to engage the collective intelligence and enthusiasm of a much larger group. A key component is that the consultant uses the relationships and trust he or she builds to obtain a more profound understanding of the issues, rather than accepting information at its face value. The process consultant will therefore look for the underlying causes of a problem, rather than the symptoms with which it manifests itself; he or she will listen as much as talk – and analytical consulting is very much about talking to clients – and will explore lateral options rather than following through a pre-specified framework.

It is an approach which is clearly suited to confused and complex situations, the nature of which cannot be captured by conventional data sources. During the course of an assignment, the process consultant is able to access more sources of data (many of which will be informal) as well as gauge the views of people within the client organisation – both of which aspects are crucial to the success of difficult assignments.

Process consulting has proved invaluable over the past decade as it has been seen as the profession's response to the frequent criticism that consultants do not engage constructively with client organisations and impose preconceived ideas on very different situations. It has also allowed consultants to deal with much more complex and lengthy assignments than pure analytical consulting would. There are, however, some significant drawbacks to this approach:

- Process consulting is highly subjective: it supplements objective data with the personal impressions of a consultant, and these may unduly influence the outcome of an assignment. Subjective input is also more difficult to defend to clients and can mean that the consultant's recommendations are dismissed.

- Some aspects of process consulting – discussing with the clients the emotions or motivation which may give rise to problems within their organisation, for example – are not dissimilar from counselling. For the untrained consultant, there is a danger that questions of these sorts may point to problems which are beyond the consultant's power to help resolve (personal problems of the client, for example): by airing such issues but leaving them unresolved, the consultant may be making an already bad situation worse.

- Clients feel – quite rightly – that they want to get value for money from consultants. Often – and this is an unfortunate repercussion – this translates into the consultant providing new information or telling an organisation to do something; it neglects the softer side of consulting where the consultant may be working with a client's own staff to help them develop a solution which they can accept. Thus, process consulting may inadvertently expose an assignment team to the charge that they have not contributed anything tangible to the organisation.

In the 'ideal' consulting assignment, because of the strengths and weaknesses of each model, fact- and process-based consulting would occur together in an optimum ratio – an equilibrium of the two styles that is precisely tailored to the needs of the individual problem faced. In practice, however, the proportions have varied more in line with the culture and working styles of the individual consulting firms, than as a result of a conscious analysis of client needs. While a minority of consulting firms have managed to balance the two effectively, the majority have tended to be biased towards one approach. The signs are that it will become more difficult for any firm to achieve this balance.

Why? The first reason is that action-based consulting has been gradually metamorphosing: with the drawbacks to the process model described above, the emphasis has been gradually shifting towards consulting firms 'doing' more – primarily in the form of outsourcing. This takes the 'doing' involved in process consulting to a new extreme in which the 'process' aspects of the consulting assignment are subordinated to the 'doing'. There is no need, in an outsourced arrangement, to spend time in transferring knowledge from the consultancy to the client, because the client will never be directly engaged in the process, only in its overall management. But, at the same time that this is happening, there is the trend among clients to demand more ideas more often and to see instantaneous results – a trend which will inexorably lead to analytical assignments (there will not be time for process; process does not deliver instant results). Moreover, other factors are likely to reinforce this trend, not least the greater availability of objective data (from information technology).

What we have, therefore, is an industry in which the pressures from clients will be pulling in two diametrically opposed directions. One trend leads to more fact-based consultancy, the other to (a now, with the emergence of outsourcing, much more extreme model of) action-based assignments. This is a very different pattern from the one which characterised the growth of the consulting industry in the past – where the trend has been, relatively consistently, from fact-based to action-based consultancy (Figure 11.1). Conventional process consulting – effectively the bridge between the two forms which maintained the balance between them – will either disappear, as the market moves in two opposing directions, or be significantly reduced.

At a high level, the impact of this does not seem overly significant. Since the shift towards action-based consultancy occurred in the 1970s, most firms have always maintained a bias towards one side or the other. Thus, by dividing consulting work more clearly between fact-based and action-based, this trend will only be making more visible a demarcation which is already present in the industry. Strategy houses will tend to do only fact-based consultancy; firms that focus on IT-related consultancy will find it increasingly difficult to win fact-based work; clients will tend to pigeon-hole firms into one style or the other. The larger firms, in order to ensure that they continue to have access to both potentially lucrative markets, will probably try to divide their organisations into fact-based and action-based consultancies and build up separate brands.

However, look below the surface, and the implications of the disappearance of process-based consultancy are much more serious. From a commercial viewpoint, process assignments have three fundamental advantages to consulting firms:

- They provide the time and money for consulting firms to develop their intellectual capital;
- They are the single most important means by which consulting firms can build and cement the relationships they have with their clients; and
- They enable the consulting labour market to stay highly flexible.

It is probably confirming every client's worst suspicions to say that consultants use billable work to develop services which can then be sold profitably to other clients. But, rationally, we have to accept that consultants will inevitably learn from their assignments and it would be foolish to prevent this learning being applied elsewhere. After all, we accept that a chair-maker's skill in making chairs is likely to rise with the number of chairs he has made. The issue, therefore, is one of acceptable balance: we do not want to buy a poorly made chair by an inexperienced craftsman, any more than we want to hire inexperienced consultants, but we should accept that, if we hire an experienced person (whether chair-maker or consultant), that person will gain further experience as the result of our hiring.

Process consulting plays an essential role in developing the experience of consultants. It allows them to go into an assignment with some knowledge of a generic process and apply that to a client's specific situation. As a result, the consultant gains both further knowledge about the process (particularly how it can be applied in the client's sector or in the context of certain issues) and an in-depth understanding of the client's own business and industry. Both types of knowledge can be reused with later clients. Moreover, it is comparatively rare that consulting firms decide to develop a new service on their own initiative. One of the advantages of working as closely with the market as they do is that consultants can be very quick to identify new clients as they emerge. It is often, for example, only with working with an actual client that a consulting firm realises that there is a wider need across a particular market.

But if clients are going to expect consultants to have a prepared solution (and this will be true of both fact-based consultancy and outsourcing), then the opportunity for consultancies to use assignments to create and develop intellectual capital will be very limited. On a wider scale, this will make it difficult for consultancy firms to evolve: what we are more likely to see is firms effectively getting stuck in different areas, unable to move from service to service as markets and clients develop. Like manufacturers, consultancies aim to move from product to product as each one passes through the traditional stages of a product life-cycle – early adoption, mass take-up, maturity and decline. But, in this scenario, firms will find it more difficult to abandon a product as it starts to decline and shift to another which is starting to take off.

Practice *versus* Theory

There are two primary drivers pushing the consulting industry away from the theorisation of its foundations to a much more hands-on way of working.

The first of these is the nature of consulting work itself. There appears to be no foreseeable let-up in the extent to which IT dominates the consulting industry. As in the past, this will continue to put consultants under pressure to do, rather than advise. Outsourcing continues to be the most obvious example of this, as it continues to expand along two distinct dimensions – the increasing levels of responsibility to which outsourcing companies are now committed, and the breadth of functions which are now considered legitimate areas for outsourcing.

A second pressure for practice over theory is the level of fees typically charged by consulting firms. High fee rates continue to encourage clients to demand more tangible results, and this typically involves more doing: consultants may have devised the most efficient shovelling systems imaginable, but – to meet their clients' expectations – they will have no choice but to pick up shovels themselves. Of course, justifying large fees by acting as well as advising is a two-way process. Consultants will be forced to 'do', in order to obtain a high fee, but they will also increasingly command high fees by offering to 'do'. Of all the trends which are likely to increase the doing to advising ratio, it is this last point which is the most important. It will be in their own interests, as much as their clients', for consultants to 'do' more and 'advise' less. In an industry in which – as we have seen – investment is becoming crucial to long-term survival, the money to be gained from 'doing' may represent the difference between success and failure. Consultancy has always involved balancing two potentially conflicting sets of objectives – the client's and the consultant's. Although clients continue to be suspicious that consultants' only interest is in raising the biggest possible bill, significant problems have been avoided by recognising that both sides stand to win or lose together.

Management Consultancy in the 21st Century identified four distinct stages in the evolution of the shift from 'advising' to 'doing', each of which it illustrated in relation to a fictional client-consultant relationship

Stage 1 – The consultant as adviser; the client as doer

The client is a medium-sized retailer operating a large number of drugstores across the country. The company has been losing market share in one of its core lines – over-the-counter healthcare products – as the supermarket chains have gradually encroached on its traditional territory and tempted loyal customers away with the discounts they can afford to give because of the economies of scale they achieve. If this company were to ask a consulting firm to work with it, the resulting assignment would look something like this. About 20 per cent of the time would be spent on market analysis, establishing the size of the healthcare market, and the opportunities and threats faced by the retailer. Probably about 40 per cent would be given over to interviews, workshops and brainstorming sessions in which the consultants bring together people with different expertise from across the client's business and facilitate a discussion between them. The aim would be for both consultants and clients to work together to develop a new approach to this particular category. Once agreement had been reached on the strategic issues, the remainder of the assignment would be given over to developing the implementation plan, identifying organisational changes or resource shortages, and other such operational areas.

Clearly, this type of assignment is vastly more hands-on than the hit-and-run tactics of which consultants are so often accused. However, it still falls short of actually 'doing' anything.

Stage 2 – The consultant and client as both adviser and doer

The same assignment – but at a different stage in the evolution of the advising to doing shift – might look something like this.

The client's objectives would probably be stated differently: rather than asking for assistance, the company would be looking for a specific result, increasing their market share in the healthcare sector by a given percentage, for example. It would then hire a consultancy to do this. This time, only a small proportion of the assignment would be given over to the traditional consulting activities – analysis, knowledge transfer, facilitation. An approach and plan would still have to be developed, but there would be no need to ensure that the client's own staff 'owned' the process, as they would not be responsible for implementing it. Moreover, there will be a positive disincentive to including the client's staff, because they will represent an unknown quantity – a risk which could jeopardise the success of the assignment.

Most of the 'assignment' would, therefore, be given over to carrying out the actions identified. Realistically, a single consulting firm is unlikely to be able to provide all the skills and resources required. One of the key secondary implications of the growing demand from clients for 'doing' will be the need for consulting firms to form consortia bids with other companies (which in this case might include an advertising agency, a database marketing company, even a manufacturer of healthcare products). The structure of the assignment, together with contractual issues and payment terms, would therefore be significantly more complex than for its equivalent today.

Stage 3 – The consultant as doer; the client as adviser

We can see how this will work by taking our hypothetical drugstore example a stage further. Suppose that the consultancy consortium has now completed the assignment successfully: the client's market share in this key category has been restored to its former dominance. Suppose also that the consortium, with some input from the client, developed a particular direct marketing tool, software which was very effective at identifying the propensity of individual consumers to buy.

Rather than leaving the tool with the client, it will make much more sense in the future to try to sell the tool on to other clients. After all, the original client has already achieved its goal (increase in market share) and its own staff may have little use for the tool on an ongoing basis – assuming that the consultancy consortium continues to manage the category once the assignment proper has finished. Clearly the drugstore retailer will want to ensure that the same tool is not sold to its direct competitors, but there would be little conflict of interest in, say, amending it for the home improvement market. Thus, a new consortium may be formed, this time involving the client, to take and develop the tool for other markets.

In this scenario, the client and consultant have effectively swapped positions, with the consultant doing the lion's share of the work and client proffering expert advice as required.

Stage 4 – The consultant as owner

To take our drugstore example one stage further again. It may be, as a result of the success of the consulting assignment and the client's burgeoning market share, that the company decides to launch a new company, perhaps specialising in the manufacture of certain types of over-the-counter healthcare products, products for which the assignment showed there was clear demand but relatively restricted supply. As a fledging business, the new manufacturer may need but be unable to afford consultancy advice. The consulting firm meanwhile sees a great opportunity about to be lost. To exploit the opportunity, the consulting firm offers to run the company in return for a portion of equity.

Of course, all four stages happen in the market simultaneously: every client, every consulting firm is at a different point in its individual evolution, each has its own limits of what it is prepared to tolerate. What is apparent, is that the 'stage 4' deals as a proportion of the total have risen considerably since the end of the 1990s, fuelled partly by a rush on the part of many firms to earn the kind of returns being enjoyed by investors up until the NASDAQ crash in April 2000. Some of these deals were in dot.coms, some of which have since failed, but many others were in the spun-out companies from large corporations. From the perspective of the latter, there's no reason to suppose that the demise of the former will change the principle now established: once consultants have accepted that they are willing to commit time and/or financial resources to a venture, why should they stop? Indeed, it's likely that clients won't let them stop, as these are the kinds of commitments which they have been seeking for some time. E-business pushed many consulting firms into the type of risk/reward-sharing partnerships with clients that they had balked at previously, and there's no way, now, that these firms can put the clock back.

The bifurcation of the consulting industry

So where does this leave consultants? I'd argue that it points to a major schism opening up within the industry. On the one side, you have consulting firms whose services and style of working tends towards 'fact-based' consulting. These are also firms whose strength will continue to lie in analysing their facts in order to create 'theories' capable of being applied from client to client, and from industry to industry. On the other side will be the 'process-based' firms, whose style and inclination will inevitably pull them towards 'practice' rather than 'theory'. As these firms evolve, taking ever more substantial stakes in their clients' ventures, the lines between themselves and their clients will dissolve. At the same time, clients that launch their own consulting ventures – as so many are now doing – are likely to position these in this same space, where practice and process predominate (Figure 9.2).

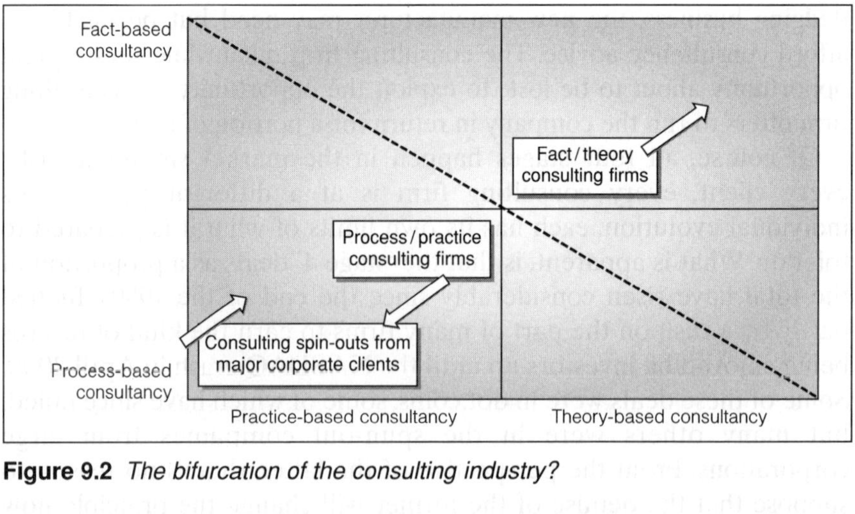

Figure 9.2 *The bifurcation of the consulting industry?*

The fact/theory model is clearly 'consulting' in its conventional sense: the question is, is the practice/process model 'consulting', and does it matter?

10

Globalisation – Panacea or Delusion?

Diversity *versus* Flexibility

Caught up in the apparent backlash against e-business and – in many cases – with declining revenues from e-business related consultancy, many consulting firms have turned to geographic expansion as a more promising source of growth. Thus, US-based firms, who were the first to feel the effects of shrinking demand, looked to the European market, where the enthusiasm for e-business seemed initially undented. As the cold wind of change moved on, UK-based firms looked to southern Europe for the same reasons, and European firms looked to the Far East.

Such moves to protect the income of consulting firms, have been reinforced by cost considerations. The recession of the early 1990s first highlighted the extent to which having a genuinely global network of resources allowed a firm to move consultants out of areas or markets which were recession-hit and into more buoyant economies. This is the model that many strategy houses have used for decades. Here, the worldwide sharing of resources is underpinned by transnational profit-sharing: thus, when one part of the world is in recession, the firm can refocus on regions which are less affected; if there is a problem with one country, it is in the interests of all the countries to resolve it. Moreover, much of the infrastructure required by consulting firms to support expansion (intellectual capital, knowledge-sharing, technology, and so on) is already proving highly expensive: pooling investment across countries has become a fundamental means by which the capital is raised for future expenditure of this nature.

There are two requisites to achieving economies of scale: a flexible workforce, not only capable of working in different countries, but of moving from service to service as the global markets for consultancy evolves; and homogeneity – both in terms of the work force (one consultant can easily do the work of another) and services (little retraining is required from one service to another). *Management Consultancy in the 21st Century* suggested that culture would be the major obstacle for consulting firms trying to achieve these economies of scale. This is because the cultural shift which should underpin the process of globalisation is not about 'simply' switching from one culture to another, perhaps from having a national, comparatively closed environment to having a much more open operation. It is about switching from having one dominant culture to accepting multiculturalism – 'legitimising diversity' in the words of the authors of *Managing Across Borders*, Christopher Bartlett and Sumantra Ghoshal Ghoshal's words. According to their estimation, the management of successful 'transnational' companies

> not only recognised the importance of the complex and changeable external forces affecting operations, but tried to reflect those characteristics internally through the development of an organization with multi-dimensional perspectives.[1]

There is evidence that some consulting firms are beginning to see diversity as a virtue. 'We're the mirror image of our clients,' commented one partner I spoke to. 'Just as many of them are trying to integrate old and new cultures without losing the best of both, we're attempting to build a company around the notion of heterogeneity, rather than homogeneity, as has been the norm in the consulting industry since its inception. That means that we've created a structure that allows for more individual autonomy and where people can develop professionally in the way they want to, not in the way we tell them we have to. We're not trying to reduce everything down to the same common denominator.'

But these are exceptions that prove the rule – and largely remain confined to the new firms, many of which are also less profitable (at the time of writing) than their more established rivals. Culture is a potential obstacle for consulting firms because flexibility and diversity are not necessarily the same things – tempting though it is to see them as such. The flexibility of consultancy, in which an assignment for one client can be analysed into rational, discrete 'methodologies' that can subsequently be applied to other clients, is the quintessential product of the Anglo-Saxon economies. Other – notably continental European and Far Eastern – economies place much greater emphasis on integration (rather than fragmentation through analysis), experience (rather than method) and community (rather than individual). As Charles Hampden-Turner and Fons Trompenaars argue in *The Seven Cultures of Capitalism*:

> The whole consultant culture is American; the very idea of sending a wise individual to mend a group is an individualistic concept.[2]

In fact, flexibility and diversity are mutually exclusive, so far as consulting firms are concerned. In order to continue meeting client needs – in order to continue to be flexible – consulting firms need some degree of operational coherence. Think how difficult it is to pull together a team of consultants, not all of whom speak English as a first language. Now overlay this with the idea of bringing together people who have very different preconceptions about, say, organisational redesign. The process by which a consulting firm responds to clients' needs – their flexibility – has to become slower as a result. This is because the flexibility of a consulting firm does not come from taking a pre-existing idea and changing it, but from pulling together several pre-existing ideas into a new synergistic whole and one which meets the needs of an individual client better than any one idea in isolation. Consultancies win assignments – usually – because they can integrate their ideas more effectively than their rivals, not because they are more innovative. Clearly, globalisation should provide a wider, much richer source of ideas that can be pulled together for clients – indeed, this is essentially the benefit that firms are seeking when they go down the globalisation road. But there is a real risk of anarchy: consultancies will have more ideas from which to choose, but less ideological coherence – fewer 'rules' – about how they should be integrated. Why should a French approach to an issue be any better than, say, a Korean?

Yet, for all this, the globalisation strategies pursued by the majority of firms remain focused on building homogeneity, not diversity; on flexibility, not difference. You build a successful firm in one country and you try to reproduce that success in another by taking with you your original organisational structure, processes and culture.

Going Local, not Global

The rationale for homogeneous expansion remains the same as it was ten years ago. John Harris, interviewed in 1991 when he was European President of Booz-Allen & Hamilton, explained that their strategy was based on a recognition that:

> our clients were moving into pan-European markets, that globalisation was an emerging management issue and that our ability to provide technology and implementation services was a basis for competitive differentiation. Our response to this situation involves operating on a pan-European basis, assigning industry and functional specialists to client teams and drawing upon resources in the US and around the world. One of our priorities is to concentrate on clients who are global competitors.[3]

Globalisation has been a source of growth for consulting firms. Clients looked to consultancy firms to provide the skills and knowledge to give them a competitive edge in their global markets. With technology, political and regulatory environments changing radically (European Monetary Union being a good example), consultancy firms were able to develop multiple service lines around the strategic and operational implications. Globalisation became a question of credibility: how could a consulting firm advise a global client if it was not global itself?

Such is the accepted wisdom within the consulting industry: but is it still valid?

Going back to talk to clients about their needs over the last couple of years reveals a significantly different picture. It's not that geographical coverage isn't still high on the corporate agenda: it still is. In fact, one of the lessons from e-business has been the need for any new venture – whether it is a start-up company or an initiative launched by an established corporation – to think global at a very early stage – far earlier than would have been the case for such a business pre-e-business. The factors driving this change appear to be twofold. There is the increasing globalisation of products and information, which allow consumers to compare goods and prices from different suppliers, as well as identifying specific items from specialised suppliers. But, at the same time, there is the fact that consumers still prefer to make their actual purchase from suppliers near to home. The message seems to be: shop global, but buy local. It has therefore become incumbent on business to promote services and products internationally, but to provide national sales and customer service functions – the virtual world only goes so far.

For small, new businesses, the challenge is to set up operations in several different countries at a stage in their evolution when, in conventional, pre-e-business terms, they would still be focusing on their first domestic market. Particularly for niche suppliers, the economies of scale necessary to success may only be obtainable by addressing several countries at once, leaving them with no option but to grow parallel organisations. 'Where we need help', commented one entrepreneur I spoke to, 'is in setting up operations in different countries. We need practical help – local agents, if you will, who'll find offices, recruit staff, strike deals on our behalf.' In fact, it's not just the smallest companies which need this kind of assistance: as large corporations create specialist spin-offs, they've been finding that their international expertise and infrastructure, while effective in supporting their existing operations, may not be designed for the new company, and that new expertise and a different infrastructure is required. 'Even though we'd been spun off from a major corporation', said one executive, 'that didn't mean that we got access to endless resources, or, indeed, the right kind of resources for our purposes'.

In terms of using consultancy, these companies – small and large – need two types of help. First, they need advice in designing their international strategy, ensuring that it has the flexibility and scalability to be applied to one country or several. Second, they need practical assistance in establishing their physical presence in different parts of the world. Neither of these, I'd argue, provides a sustainable rationale for the homogeneous model pursued by the majority of large consulting firms, and it may at least partly account for why one of the predictions of *Management Consultancy in the 21st Century*, that a new breed of professional service firms – the 'global super firms' – would emerge, has not been fulfilled in reality.

I argued that it was already becoming apparent that the costs of complete integration – people, processes, systems, strategy, and marketing – would be unacceptably high in many instances. A more incremental approach was needed, one which prioritised specific areas for investment. Some services would become more global than others. One firm might, for example, choose to make its pharmaceutical practice global, but leave its banking practice on a national footing; another might prefer to pin its global hopes on cross-sector corporate transformation, but manage process improvement assignments locally. Ahead of a full-scale transnational structure, these chosen services would have global resources and targets – they would, in effect, form a core of new, 'super' services. This process was clearly linked to that of increased specialisation in that there would be a tendency for each firm to pick global specialisations which would differentiate it from its competitors. Over time, as these new services grew and acquired an established reputation, the overall positioning of consulting firms would become more differentiated, reducing the high level of generic competition which has bedevilled the industry to date.

Part of the reason why this didn't happen was internal. Two years ago, I argued that a further effect would be the emergence of a division between global and national services. Global services would inevitably be the areas of high market profile and strong investment; they would attract and retain the best people. From feeling slightly neglected in the first instance, national services would begin to be marginalised. Success would feed success, and failure, failure. As the global services recruited better people, they would deliver better assignments and attract more clients; this would in turn boost recruitment, and the virtuous circle would continue. By contrast, national services would be pulled into a downward spiral, as they continually lose their best people to their global counterparts. Internal conflict would grow, at least until the inevitable was recognised – that the global and national services constitute two separate firms, the former focused on international clients in a limited range of sectors, the latter offering much more generic services to a domestic market, concentrating on clients with no or little international aspirations.

While I think these comments remain true, what I underestimated was the extent to which they were recognised by individual consultants, perhaps unconsciously. Faced with this kind of scenario, no consultant in his or her right mind would want to be associated with a 'national' practice. Inevitably – and certainly where partnership structures have allowed a degree of personal autonomy – everyone began to position themselves as global players. You could tell senior partners apart from junior ones, based on the geographical coverage of their position: at the lowest rung in the ladder were country-specific partners; next, half-way up the ladder, were partners whose responsibilities covered a group of countries; then, at the top, were the global service line or sector leaders. A degree of fall-out was apparent, but this applied particularly to other professional services – notably audit – which had long been bracketed with consultancy but now found itself constrained by the national differences in regulation and disclosure.

But, beyond such internal factors, there's increasing evidence from clients that the one-firm model may not suit their needs, either for strategic advice or for more practical help.

Taking strategic advice first: most clients would admit that they need help in drawing up their international strategy. According to one client: 'one of the major benefits of having access to consultants has been that it gave us the opportunity to discuss issues which we might otherwise have put off. Although we – like everyone else – had announced our intention to be a global player, we hadn't given our strategy for doing this much serious attention. If anything, we thought: "we'll develop our initial operation in this country, then roll it out to others". It was the consultancy firm who demonstrated to us that it was complex and helped develop our approach.' 'It's not just a question of the idea itself', commented another, 'but the extent to which the business model behind it can be replicated in different countries without becoming prohibitively complex and expensive ... You can be a successful company in one country, only to discover that people buy your services differently in another. Gathering information on these differences and assimilating the conclusions takes time.'

But the fact that they require strategic advice on globalisation, doesn't necessarily mean that they need a global firm to give it to them. Quite the reverse, in fact. 'Looking for help in developing our international strategy, isn't so very different to looking for any other form of consultancy', said one executive. 'We're always looking for the same things – specialisation and world-class expertise. If we find that there's a real expert in a market that we're considering entering based in – say – the Far East, then it's that expert we want, not his or her colleagues based locally. We prefer to go where the expertise is, and we certainly don't assume that, just because a particular firm has an office round the corner from us, that the people in that office will be equipped to help on a particular issue. It's exactly the same whatever the specialist input is that we're seeking.' Indeed, globalisation is in danger of being tarred by the same brush that has blackened the reputation of one-stop-shopping: 'just because a consulting firm has an outpost in every country, doesn't mean that they'll have the skills we need in that country', said another. 'In fact, we tend to be suspicious when consulting firms tell us they're global: it's like saying they're a jack of all trades, but a master of none. It's just not credible to claim that you have the same level of expertise in all places and, once you've accepted that, then it's only a short step to say that you've got 'centres of excellence' in different parts of the world. That's not globalism, but it's a sensible and credible allocation of resources.'

Moving on to the more practical help that clients are increasingly looking to outsiders – often consultants – to provide, it's clear that clients are looking to buy heterogeneity here – that is an understanding of local market conditions and cultural differences – not global similarity. As one consultant I talked to summarised the situation, 'it's not enough to offer advice about the country or market a company is trying to enter – you have to be able to start the ball rolling. For example, one of our clients was looking to expand into the European market, so one of our French partners became the interim CEO and was responsible for setting up the French operation from scratch in six weeks, including selecting and negotiating with the strategic partners who had to be involved, putting the legal structure in place, recruiting, finding offices and sorting out many of the logistical issues involved in start-ups.' A key role for consultants, therefore, is to be able to go beyond the strategy development process by providing points of contact in different physical locations: in effect, to be the network of new organisation before it has had the opportunity to build one of its own.

Over the last ten years, the consulting industry has become polarised between two models of international structure. On the one hand, there is the large, established firm, capable of gathering information and offering consulting support at a local level, while simultaneously offering a single, consistent approach, that has dominated the consulting industry for the last two decades. Although such firms may have grown out of different national firms, they have already left, or aspire to leave, their heterogeneous origins behind. On the other hand are the newer firms whose structures still reflect the networks of locally based consultancies from which they have developed and who have no intention of creating a single, homogenous structure.

The greater geographical reach of the post-e-business environment would appear, at first sight, to favour the first of these models. However, such a conclusion would be premature: although it undoubtedly creates an opportunity for consulting firms to help research and develop strategies on their clients' behalf, it's questionable whether that translates into a need for firms to have a *consulting* presence in multiple countries, as the global model has presumed. Most of the clients I've talked to, who've made use of consultants in researching and/or developing their international strategy, used specialists – pulled in from wherever in the world they were based, so that the actual consulting always happened at home. Where they drew on the international network of these firms, it was purely to gather information. One of the flaws of the 'global presence theory' is that a business in one country does not necessarily want consultancy input in another: local people, getting the business off the ground, are much more important.

The global, homogeneous consulting organisation may have had its day.

[1] Christopher Bartlett and Sumantra Ghoshal, *Managing Across Borders: The Transnational Solution* (London: Century Business, 1992), p. 209.

[2] Charles Hampden-Turner and Fons Trompenaars, *The Seven Cultures of Capitalism: Value Systems for Creating Wealth in the United States, Britain, Japan, Germany, France, Sweden and The Netherlands* (New York: Doubleday), 1993, p. 61.

[2] Quoted in Charles Rassam and David Oates, *Management Consulting: The Inside Story* (London: Mercury, 1991), p. 88.

11

Creating the Consulting Brand Experience

I'm constantly amazed when I walk into a bullish new consultancy, confident in its ability to succeed in a market in which so many new entrants have failed, when the founders talk about 'adding value' to clients and 'working in partnership' with them. Do they really think that there's something unique in this? Haven't they read the marketing literature of almost every other consulting firm on the planet?

It continues to be the case that consultants try hard to mirror their clients – by 'working in partnership' with them, by trying to anticipate and meet their needs, and so on. This imitative, rather than innovative, behaviour, applies at both the micro and macro level. When several consultancies decide to bid for a specific assignment, they attempt to tailor their way of working to the client's individual needs (indeed, one of the most common sources of client dissatisfaction is that consultants do not do this enough). In their effort to win the work involved, the approaches adopted by the different consulting firms inevitably start to converge: the bigger the assignment, the greater the formality with which client needs are laid out, and the more likely it is that convergence will take place. At the more macro level, the intangible nature of consultancy services breeds similarity. BPR would not be BPR if the only two firms offering it as a service approached assignments very differently. Consulting firms still have to deal with peculiarly inelastic product definitions: it does not take much to stretch the BPR process into something that would not be conceived of as BPR.

Moreover, there's little short-run incentive for consulting firms to break out of this situation. Homogeneous products can be altered and recycled relatively quickly and easily (hence the criticisms that BPR was just traditional cost-reduction consultancy in a new guise). Innovation is both expensive and risky: it makes much more economic sense for consulting firms to prevent the markets for services becoming fragmented by reaching some degree of consensus about what this service should look like. Of course, each firm will develop and promote its individual variations on the central theme, but the core product will be – has to be – the same. Although barriers to entry and levels of investment are rising, they are still low compared to most other industries: establishing a service 'definition' will provide established players with a modicum of protection, as it creates a standard which new entrants have to match. In the short-term, therefore, the vast majority of incumbents in the consulting industry benefit from collaboration (even if it's undertaken unconsciously), rather than competition – as the preceding chapter points out. It's only in the long term, that standing out from the crowd may offer a sustainable competitive advantage.

To be fair to the new entrants: if differentiation was an easy problem to solve, they – indeed, all firms – would have solved it long ago. But, as it is, we're stuck with the situation I commented on in the original edition of this book: that differentiation is one of the most serious issues facing the consulting industry, driven by the need of consulting firms to strengthen client loyalty – witness the multi-million dollar campaign launched by newly-named Accenture in January 2001.

If anything, e-business has made this problem more complicated. Take, for example, some of the comments I've encountered when interviewing clients:

- 'I used to know how to buy consultancy – who to call in for what project – but the explosion of new firms and new technologies on the market has meant that I don't know who to turn to, especially when we're moving outside our own areas of expertise.'
- 'We asked several companies to pitch for the business, and were astonished when they all claimed to have been involved in the same seminal project undertaken by one of our competitors. Surely they can't all have been working on the same engagement?'
- 'You have to think of buying consultancy in terms of the intellectual capital you're trying to acquire: otherwise you can end up reinventing a wheel you already have and demoralising your own people. But consulting firms don't make this process any easier. They won't – or can't – articulate their intellectual assets with sufficient precision: the detail is lost in the overall message of the brand.'

While e-business may have made the problem harder to solve, it has – I'd argue – made its underlying nature clearer. The problem is not simply one of differentiation, it's one of access to information, and of how information relates to the broader issues concerned with brand. Furthermore, e-business has also changed our thinking about customer loyalty: so many dot.coms appear to have failed because they focused on enabling their customers to perform online transactions, not in building long-term relationships with them:

> In the online economy, relationship is all. Transactions are almost literally nothing. The transaction player has to pay out more to get the customer than what its average sale makes for it ... It loses money on every deal. The relationship player also has to spend money to attract customers. But it recovers that investment by building repeat business, adding new products and services through acquisition and alliances, and collecting referral fees ... The relationship leader deepens the customer link through personalization, customization, dynamic interaction, collaboration and building community.[1]

In an increasingly networked economy, in which the distinction between client and consultant is becoming more and more blurred (see Chapters 2 and 9), relationship building may not simply increase client loyalty, but may provide an opportunity to establish genuine competitive advantage. I'd argue that being able to build an effective relationship with a client is based on both brand 'experience' and information: the problem for consulting firms is that these two things are often treated as mutually exclusive.

Building a Consulting Brand Experience

One of the paradoxical ways in which e-business has changed the consulting industry is that it has made it – simultaneously – less and more 'real'.

'Less real' in the sense that clients no longer wanted theory, they wanted action: they didn't want a consultant who'd got 20 years of experience in advising – say – the retail industry; they wanted someone who'd got 20 weeks' experience in running an online business. With so much earlier thinking being thrown out with the bath-water, a hands-on background, however short, was the key to client credibility. Moreover, clients' own experiences justified this shift: 'I've learnt more in the three months I've been running this company than I did over three years as a consultant', commented the CEO of one dot.com I spoke to. At the same time, the new e-specialists were receiving a boost from clients who wanted to buy a different style of consulting – one in which the process matched the new economy content. 'Clients', said one of these firms, 'come to us because they want the project to feel different to previous consulting projects; they don't want the procedures and endless bureaucracy they've often come to associate with consultants, but something more informal.' According to a client: 'when we hire one of these new firms, it's partly because we want our people to experience a different way of working, one that's quite different to that which they're accustomed to. We treat projects like this as pilots for how we want to work in the future.'

Consulting firms have responded to this threat to their core – primarily theoretical – identity – by trying to make themselves appear more 'real'. This has taken several forms – of which the trend towards launching their own businesses, discussed in the previous chapter is just one. But perhaps the most significant of these has been to rethink what the consulting process feels like from a client perspective, and to appreciate that this type of 'experience' plays a fundamental role in an engagement as a whole. In line with companies in other sectors, consulting firms have begun to appreciate that their brand is not simply about advertising, but the consistency with which it can 'walk the talk'.

The traditional approach to differentiation within the consulting industry has been specialisation. It has, for example, been by emphasising their new ideas or in-depth experience in a particular field that new entrants have been successful in carving out niches for themselves. Established, broader-based firms have responded in kind, typically by promoting specific services: 'growth through specialisation' became the strategy of more than one consultancy in the early 1990s.

But there are two major problems with the idea of using specialisation to differentiate.

The first is that specialisation itself does nothing to promote a brand: rather the opposite, it leads to fragmentation. Time and money have been spent designing frameworks which bring these different elements together, but the exercise is a structural one – the whole never adds up to more than the sum of the parts. For many companies, this external image has been the mirror image of internal fragmentation, with firms split into a myriad of separate business units, each of which is pursuing a quasi-autonomous strategy. Without clear internal goals and values, it has been almost impossible to develop a more coherent external image, let alone a brand.

The second problem is that the specialisms that are being used as a source of differentiation are prone to change. Everyone – consultants and clients alike – would recognise that consultancy is, and has to be, a fast-moving business. Intellectual capital does not require the massive R&D budgets of, say, a pharmaceutical company; nor does it – unlike a car manufacturer, for example – need a huge assembly line to be constructed. In order to operate effectively in the intellectual capital market, consulting firms need to be immensely responsive to changes in their clients' demands, and fragmentation is one way of dealing with this issue. Large, hierarchical firms are like oil tankers – once set in a direction, they take time to change course. By contrast, an organisation that is composed of many small units, each of which is very focused on their immediate markets, can change course much more quickly. Of course, the downside is that the fragmented organisation is less good at moving in a single direction – which is part of the explanation why more fragmentary organisations are less effective when it comes to a stable environment. Consultancies, therefore, need to change their specialisms in order to survive, but, as a result, it becomes difficult for the specialist image being promoted to add up to a sustainable brand.

It is one of the axioms of marketing that intangible services are most effectively promoted via tangible substitutes. Thus, rather than tell us how good their people are, the reports of consulting firms have tended to give us pictures of real people; equally, rather than just claiming that their assignments have yielded positive results, they have shown real clients talking about real benefits. But the process has tended to stop there: very few consulting firms have managed to create any more substantial an impression, or any more concrete a brand. Indeed, simply because these firms have relied on people – staff and clients – to embody the brand, there is a limit to the extent to which the values they are trying to embody will appear different. People – especially in written reports – tend to sound and look the same. Thus, not only (as we observed earlier) are the propositions of consulting firms undifferentiated, but so are the mechanisms which they adopt to promote them.

More recently, consulting firms have begun to see that the knowledge that these people have – the firm's intellectual capital – is also an asset. Business books, journals and articles have already become some of the most important weapons in the consultant's armoury, and will continue to be so in the future. Many of the largest consulting firms are attempting to secure their position on the intellectual high ground by launching their own journals and by allying themselves to specific business schools in order to gain access to a constant source of research material. A combination of increased investment and more intense competition for this intellectual high ground will mean that consulting firms have to become considerably more focused in terms of promoting their intellectual assets. For the minority of firms already trying to exploit this opportunity at the moment, air time is allocated pretty much on a first-come-first-served basis, with comparatively little thought being put into promoting a firm's key intellectual assets on a more systematic basis. In the future, no doubt, this will change, with consulting firms using journals, books and related media on a much more strategic basis. The fight to win a client's business will start, not at the door of their offices or on the first page of the proposal, but long before the client invites a consulting firm to bid for an assignment.

However, creating a differentiated *experiential* brand will require a different approach – one that requires considerably more than the written word in order to sustain it. It's no accident, therefore, that we've started to see consulting firms redesigning their work space, partly to take advantage of the economics of hot-desking, but also to reinforce, in physical terms, some of their marketing messages about collaboration, innovative thinking and flexible working. You could argue that the whole notion of focused 'proposition development' (discussed in Chapter 3) stemmed as much from the need to give clients a different experience as part of the consulting process, as it did from the need to find a faster means of taking new ventures to market. In fact, proposition development is significant because it suggests that consulting companies are beginning to replace conventional written methodologies, with what can only be termed 'experiential' methodologies in which much less of the process is documented, and more of it is acted out; in which much more is based around the gut instinct of the project's director than on a standardised set of procedures.

This shift to 'experiential' consulting may have been initiated by the new ways of working boasted by many dot.coms, but it is likely to outlast them, because it offers consulting firms a further defence in the continuing war – discussed in the original edition of this book – against commoditisation. *Management Consultancy in the 21st Century* argued that some of the underlying economics which had maintained the homogeneity of consulting, almost since its incept, were starting to change. The more widely a consulting service becomes available, the more likely it is to be commoditised – partly as a result of greater availability (any old consultant can do this), partly as the service definition became untenably stretched. As consulting firms become faster at gathering and acting on market intelligence, and become more efficient at developing their own, often look-alike services, so this process of commoditisation will speed up. Ten years ago, a leading-edge consultancy service had a shelf-life of perhaps five years; in 1999, two years was probably more typical; today, in 2001, e-business has made those time scales even shorter: months now, perhaps, rather than years. Experiential consulting is a key means by which a consulting firm can break out of this vicious circle – because it is the one thing 'any old consultant' will find very hard to replicate. It is also – not uncoincidentally – one of the things that a software company, attempting to convert a paper-based methodology into software, or a business services company, attempting to provide online consulting, will find hardest to deliver.

It's the first stage in the defence of the consulting industry against direct competition via electronic channels.

Brand *versus* Information?

The problem is that, while the imperative of developing an experiential brand is pushing consulting firms in one direction – away from using pure intellectual capital (in the form of management books, articles, and so on), and towards creating a brand experience – clients appear to be moving in the opposite direction. As one client put it, 'we want to be able to see exactly how a particular firm matches our needs. We start with a precise definition of what we want, and we then look to see who can provide that. The trouble is that most consulting firms don't present information this precisely: most of the marketing literature is too high-level for our purposes, but it's often difficult to get beyond it.'

What this client has put his finger on is one of the conundrums of consulting. We're accustomed to thinking of marketing literature as a window on an organisation, opening up its products and services to potential purchasers. But it is – obviously – also the picture that that organisation wants us to see and, as such, it can constitute a barrier between customers and the information they think they need. The consulting firms– almost without exception – are a good illustration of this, and it's important to recognise that much of the client purchasing process and the consultancy sales process are both driven by the underlying asymmetry of information. The reason why clients only very rarely get the information they want is that it is fundamentally not in the economic interest of consulting firms to provide it. What most clients want is a directory, telling them who specialises in what in which firm and how good they are. These two specific pieces of information (individuals' areas of expertise and ratings) form two of the most important intellectual assets of a firm. Never mind all that talk about methodologies or benchmark data: this is the intellectual capital that matters most, and without which a firm would cease to exist. After all, what other reason does a firm have to exist, unless it is to build, own and sell this information? It's what clients pay for when they buy a firm, rather than a free-lance consultant (although the latter have their own networks to facilitate matchmaking between themselves and clients, so a mechanism exists here as well). Hardly surprising, then, that consultancies don't give this information away. Think how many web-sites there are for consulting firms: how many of any but the smallest firms provide details of actual named individuals whom a client can contact directly. And ratings? This is implicit in a client's selection of a firm: one of the reasons why very large corporations use very large consulting firms is that this provides them with a measure of quality assurance – the consulting process has gone through a process of accreditation (recruitment) so the client doesn't have to. No surprise, therefore, that consulting firms continue to be spectacularly uninterested in external accreditation or developing a professional qualification for the consulting industry: doing this would pose a direct threat to the role of the firm, as clients would have both an external source of information about individual consultants and information on their quality.

So is this as far as it goes? Does this represent some sort of impasse in the client-consultant relationship, with neither side able to progress and both suffering a degree of chronic dissatisfaction?

I think the answer is 'no' for two reasons. The first of these was partially touched on in *Management Consultancy in the 21st Century*, which made the point that the majority of consulting firms had long neglected one of their most important assets – the information they held on their clients as a result of their relationships with them. It argued that, while the overall trend in the industry may be away from client loyalty on a corporate scale, almost all consultants strive to acquire and retain the trust and confidence of clients on an individual basis. That software suppliers – for example – want to forge alliances with the major consulting firms is evidence of the extent to which these relationships are enormously valuable. Consulting firms often have access to the board of a company in a way in which no software manufacturer could hope to have, and using consultants as a conduit for their products is therefore hugely important.

Attempts to realise the value of these relationships have tended to remain at the individual level – typically, a partner is asked to facilitate the introduction of a colleague to a client. But this is in stark contrast to other sectors, notably financial services and retailing, where it has been recognised that an organisation's relationship with its customers needs to be understood and exploited on a much more systematic basis. Saga, a British company which has traditionally organised holidays for retired people, has used its customer base (and their loyalty to its brand) to move into new areas such as insurance. Although they have yet to appreciate or act on it, the same applies to consulting firms. They – especially the largest, more established firms – potentially have access to a highly valuable database of contacts, areas of interest, and so on. The problem is that it currently exists only in people's heads: yes, a firm is likely to record the names and addresses of clients; yes, they may also keep a check on what client bought what service; but no firm has yet succeeded in capturing the mass of informal, unstructured knowledge about clients' likes and dislikes, future interests, career ambitions, and so on – which, collectively, represents its most valuable information on clients. Of course, many clients will not want to purchase all their consultancy from one firm, but these types of relationship marketing activities will significantly improve a firm's overall sales effectiveness.

One of the lessons of e-business is that, to capture this kind of information and automate its application cannot be a one-sided affair. Customers are willing to give suppliers extraordinarily detailed information, but only where they perceive it is in their interest to do so – and a fundamental part of the calculation people make is in terms of the information they receive back. Telling a hotel chain your room preferences makes sense if they can provide you with instant and reliable information back in return – perhaps on the availability of the type of rooms you like. The same is true of consulting firms: a client will be much more willing to participate in a firm's attempt to build up its knowledge base (for example, in terms of who's who in the organisational chart), if it thinks the consulting firm will reciprocate by providing information on its consultants: thus, individuals in both organisations will be able to make bilateral connections, without having recourse to a higher authority. Of course, some such arrangements do exist but they're hardly par for the course – at the moment. But it's a trade-off for the consulting firm: which is more valuable, cementing relationships with their clients by exchanging information, or continuing to control the flow of information by keeping it within the firm?

The second reason why the brand/experience dichotomy may change is rooted in the first. We only have to look at the experience of other industries to see how radically industries which share two characteristics – asymmetrical information and a fragmented market – can be transformed by web-enabled technologies: banking, insurance and travel are the obvious examples, but it's equally true for areas like business education. How long will business schools continue to exist? As we've just noted, information asymmetries certainly exist in the consulting marketplace, but that second characteristic – fragmentation – is just as apposite. Although dominated by a small number of large firms, the plethora of small, specialist consultancies continues to grow exponentially. Furthermore, the purchase and sale of consultancy is even more fragmented than the industry statistics would suggest, as it remains very a much a matter of individual personalities and choice.

Information has empowered consumers in other parts of the economy: there seems little reason to suppose that it will not do so in the consulting industry as well.

[1] Nick Earle and Peter Keen, *From .Com to .Profit: Inventing Business Models that Deliver Value and Profit* (San Francisco: Jossey-Bass, 2000), p. 92.

Part III
Interviews

12

Introduction to the Interviews

No one has a monopoly on the future.

While the first part of this book has focused on my own views, it's important to reflect how leading consultants across the industry see the next few years. As ever, I'm deeply grateful to the individuals who gave up their time to talk to me, and I hope the following pages do justice to their views.

Bringing all the discussions together, it's clear – and perhaps not surprising – that there is consensus about some areas, and disagreement about others. A common picture of the changing needs and behaviours of clients certainly emerges – one in which clients, increasingly precise about their consulting needs and discriminating in terms of the skills they're looking for, are much more selective. Some people foresee a world in which the majority of the largest clients have rosters of pre-qualified consultants: survival will be determined by a firm's ability to get itself on to this roster; those who fail will become expert suppliers through the channel of a branded firm, rather than have an identity of their own. Faced with these challenges, almost everyone agrees that it's the retention of existing clients that matters most, not the acquisition of new ones.

This outlook chimes with a changed perception about the industry. *Management Consultancy in the 21st Century* was written at a time when demand was growing strongly: this book, at a time when, for a variety of reasons, many of which are touched on in the following pages, the consulting industry has excess capacity and faces a shrinking market. While most of those interviewed remained bullish about the prognosis for the industry in the long term, few did not acknowledge that the short-term future may be tough, a period either of reinvention or of consolidation and retrenchment.

While everyone has a different strategy for survival and long-term success, one message comes through extremely clearly – the need for consulting firms, like their clients, to focus on their core competencies. Clients want to buy 'best-of-breed' skills: they require consulting firms to be clear about what they do best, and what they cannot do at all. The form this imperative will take will vary across the major segments of the industry. What should a firm's relationship – if any – be with the major technology suppliers? How far will – and can – a firm align itself with its clients: by risk-sharing arrangements, through 'sweat equity' deals, by taking up their cudgels and fighting for their client against the competition?

And what are the internal ramifications of these changes? Where incumbent firms acknowledge the impact of the e-business consultancies founded in the 1990s (and not all do), it's largely internally that they see a difference – in particular, the need to overcome functional boundaries in order to create teams that provide clients with genuinely integrated strategy, creative and technology skills.

But perhaps the most significant change of all – and I do think this is one that you can attribute to the new consulting firms as a group, and irrespective of the survival of any individual firm from among them – is the growing sense of visible, articulated identity among consulting firms. Ten years ago, the majority of consultancy happened behind the scenes: what e-business has done since 1998 is bring consultancy out into the open: in books and newspapers, on stock markets, as investors, at the launch parties of new ventures. And I think this is matched by the extent to which the people I spoke to were mapping out conscious, deliberate and – most importantly – overt strategies for the future: it's all a far cry from the rather vague public positioning statements of the early 1990s.

Perhaps the comments of John Donahoe at Bain & Company sum this up: 'We've done a considerable amount of research on the way in which sustainable success comes from driving the profits out of the core of your business: maybe we'll be proved wrong in the future, but, if we are wrong, then it won't be because we didn't have a point of view!'

13

American Management Systems

David Yates

American Management Systems (AMS) is an international business and information technology consulting firm that helps clients create value by increasing revenues and market share and by decreasing costs. The firm combines expertise in business analytics, business process design and information technology with a deep understanding of the industries it serves, including financial services, news media and communications, energy, healthcare and US federal, state and local government.

AMS has specialist expertise in the areas of customer relationship management; credit, market and operational risk management; eBusiness; billing and operational support systems; enterprise and B2B integration. The firm's clients are industry leading organisations and AMS derives over 85 per cent of its business each year from clients with whom the firm has worked in previous years.

Founded in 1970, AMS is headquartered in Fairfax, Virginia, with 8750 employees and 51 offices worldwide. AMS reported 2000 revenues of $1.28 bn.

David Yates is General Manager for AMS in Northern Europe with overall responsibility for all of AMS' client engagements in that area. Prior to taking on this position, he was head of AMS' Corporate Banking Practice based in New York, where he was engagement manager for a variety of high value client engagements in the area of corporate banking business process re-engineering, business case development and consulting for in- and out-sourcing of processing businesses. Yates is also a member of the Management Board and the AMS Engagement Manager for a Joint Venture between AMS, ANZ, Bank of Montreal and Barclays Bank. This venture, headquartered in Toronto and Melbourne, is positioned to become the largest processor of Trade Services worldwide. Yates has eighteen years of experience consulting to and carrying out major systems implementations for blue chip financial institutions worldwide, in which capacity he has acted as engagement manager on projects ranging in size from one year product implementations with a value of $3 million to multi-year systems integration projects in the context of corporate mergers and organisational renewal with a value in excess of $40 m.

‘The failure of even a large number of dot.com companies doesn't negate the arguments that underpin e-business: in fact, I think the ‘second round’ will emerge even more strongly as a result of the current consolidation. To date, a considerable amount has been invested in business-to-consumer models, most of which have been based on fundamentally unpredictable business propositions – as it's extraordinarily difficult to foresee how consumers are going to behave in relation to new technology. In order to tie in more solid revenue streams, activity will migrate, not so much to the business-to-business arena, but towards business-to-employee issues – productivity, self-service, more open communications.

The new consulting firms played a significant role in evangelising and legitimising the e-world, and it took some time before the incumbent players were able to respond effectively. But consultancy, like every other sector, needs an injection of new competition periodically if it's to retain its capacity to adapt to changing market conditions, and these new firms created a different benchmark for what a consulting firm could look like. It's ironic that, at the moment, just as the older firms are trying to replicate their style of organisation and culture, those firms are having to retrench and may well end up looking more like the incumbents from whom they sought to differentiate themselves.

The challenge going forward is the same for consultants as it is for their clients – how to combine the best of the ‘old’ and the ‘new’. The core strengths of AMS, for example, have lain in large transactional systems and what we have to do is understand how you combine these kinds of systems, which remain fundamental to the processes of many corporations, with the web-enabled technology now available. It's not a question of one technology superseding another: creating links between the old and the new provides us with a significant opportunity to maximise the value of both. Many companies now realise that they wasted a considerable amount of money on comparatively simple front-end technology that may make it harder for them to integrate different channels in the future and simply added a layer of cost, rather than rationalising. As a result, I think we'll see a lot of investment in the next few years in terms of changing the back office infrastructure so that it can accommodate, not just a variety of channels, but also multiple links with other organisations. We have to be careful that we don't simply replace one inflexible system with another: going forward, the onus is on the consulting firm to be more creative, both in terms of the recommendations they make and the way in which they work.

By the latter I don't necessarily mean taking equity in exchange for fees: I think clients are looking for a genuine, long-term commitment to a particular venture. There's one venture with which AMS has been involved – Proponix – which perhaps points to a way in which this will work in the future. It's a collaboration between AMS and three banks – one European, one Australian and one North American – which aims to deliver trade services to other banks. Clearly, a key component will be the capacity to handle very large volumes of transactional data, but it's such an important component – the business will be so dependent on these systems – that it didn't make sense to hire a consulting firm on a conventional basis. You have to be able to believe that the consulting firm is as heavily committed to the long-term success of the venture as the other partners. We're also playing a facilitating role: historically, banks have tended to make bilateral alliances, but ventures such as Proponix require not only more than two partners in order to acquire the critical mass to convince the markets, but a plethora of additional suppliers. In this case, because of the geographical spread of the major partners, the potential conflict of interest is minimal; but despite that, companies aren't accustomed to thinking about inter-company communication – their historical focus has been their own business. By contrast, taking ideas to different companies and different industries is one of the core capabilities of a consulting firm. The consultant therefore plays a fundamental role in ventures such as Proponix in terms of opening the venture up, of persuading traditional competitors that they may, in fact, create more value through collaboration. We make sales calls; we have Proponix business cards; we even hire other consulting firms as service providers. We had baseball caps made which say 'Proponix' on one side, and 'AMS/Bank' on the other; so we could turn them around to remember the perspective we had at a particular moment!

That being said, I don't think consulting firms will be treated as absolutely equal partners: the client-consultant distinction will remain, because we remain a 'supplier' of services into these arrangements, and the client partners will therefore always retain the ultimate veto over our presence. I also think it becomes difficult to sustain anything like an equal relationship unless you're absolutely clear about the value that you're bringing to the party. And by 'value' I really mean something that's tangible: the days when a consulting firm could survive because they have a good idea or simply have smart people have passed. In the future, consultants are going to have to contribute assets, either pre-existing intellectual content or software.

The increasing tangibility – as I'd see it – of the consulting industry has substantial ramifications. It's always been difficult to stop people leaving with good ideas, but if a greater proportion of your intellectual capital has been converted into tangible products – surveys, reports, and software – then your control over your strategic 'assets' increases – something that's going to be important in the future when consulting firms want to raise capital. Cash has never been thick on the ground in this industry, but having more defined intellectual capital is going to change investors' perception of consulting firms.

Another trend the Proponix venture illustrates is greater outsourcing of clients' back office function. While the efficiency of these may constitute a strategic asset, the majority of organisations regard them as a drain on their profitability. They see their front-end as key to differentiation, but are essentially looking for an engine which will manage their back office systems. To do this, they're beginning to recognise that they'll gain more from co-operation than competition. What worries me here is that consulting firms themselves aren't themselves particularly good examples of collaborators. We have worked together where we've seen that we have complementary skill sets, but the traditional model of consulting is that it expands to fill available vacuums, so any firm, however focused it is at the start, finds it hard to retain that focus over time. In a collaborative environment, you can't do this: you have to recognise a gap when you see one, and bring in a specialist partner, rather than try to grow a skill yourself.

This is certainly something that we're now more conscious of, having gone through the experience of building Proponix: we had to resist the temptation to say 'Oh, we could do that' and, instead, go out and find an expert firm. We've really been able to see the consulting industry from the client's perspective, and that's made us much more conscious of some issues. Because we're now the budget holders, we find ourselves being extremely clear about precisely what we are looking for from a consulting firm – and paying for that and nothing more. We're finding that our purchase of consulting skills is much more fragmented as a result; we're also clearer about when we're simply buying extra resources, and where there's specific intellectual capital we're looking for. Seeing a tendering process from the client's side of the table has brought home for us just how untenable a generic business proposition is from a consulting firm. However much a firm like this uses its knowledge management system, it can't conceal the fact that its intellectual capital has been mechanically generated: you can see that the people you meet simply haven't thought it through. As clients, we don't want to buy generic consultancy: we want the 'best of breed', and that's something that no one firm can guarantee in all areas. The most effective presentations were by consultants who could use their practical experience to bring the subject matter to life, and large consultancies with set methodologies for doing things can sometimes be a barrier, making it harder for clients to find the real experts. Even more than today, real competitive differentiation in the future will come from being able to pull out all the stops in order to make things work, and it will mean taking more genuine risks with the client. ’

14

Andersen

John Kerr

Since being established in 1913, Andersen has enjoyed uninterrupted year on year growth by developing innovative solutions which help people and organisations create and realise value. Andersen offers Business Consulting, Global Corporate Finance, Tax and Legal and Audit and Business Advisory services, with 390 offices in 84 countries and an annual revenue of more than $8.4 bn for the year to 31 August 2000.

John Kerr is Managing Partner for Business Consulting Western Europe and CEEMEIA. Kerr joined Andersen in 1978 after working in London as a strategic financial consultant; he went on to head Andersen's Business Consulting practice in his native Scotland.

He was promoted to his current post after three years as the Deputy Managing Partner, Business Consulting, UK. In that position, he was part of a team that grew the practice from £30 m to £100 m in just three years. In the spring of 2000, Kerr was also given the responsibility of furthering all of Andersen's eBusiness services in the UK, including cross-service category services in tax and legal.

‘The last couple of years have had a significant impact on the consulting industry. At the height of the e-business boom, there were a lot of arrogant consulting firms about, each effectively saying ‘the highway is my way’ – so much so that that kind of attitude became the norm, rather than the exception. The upside to all the recent failures is that it's shaken up these assumptions: however much you want to be first to market, you can't infinitely compress a consulting project; however flexible you need to be, you still need to have a clear set of objectives and deliverables. But, although so many of those pure-play e-consulting firms, which caused such an uproar, are now disappearing, we shouldn't underestimate the impact they've had, particularly in relation to how we have to motivate and reward consultants in the future. I think it's also partly as a result of these firms that clients have become much more demanding and selective.

But perhaps more than anything, e-business has exposed some significant fallacies. First, the idea of one firm being able to meet all a client's diverse needs isn't sustainable. Clients have made it abundantly clear that they want to work with the 'best of breed' in each area and aren't satisfied with firms that are, in effect, jacks of all trades, but masters of none. Second, there's the question of ownership. In the early days of e-business consulting we were being told that the partnership model was dead, but now I think we're realising that its apparent replacement – public ownership – has its own, quite considerable disadvantages. Finally, e-business has challenged the relationship between the consulting industry and technology. If you look back at the history of consulting, it's hard to avoid the conclusion that many of its protagonists have been pretty arrogant. They've made various dangerous assumptions – that, for instance, they're smarter than their clients – and have been able to live in ivory towers, comparatively remote from changes in technology. But clients are starting to turn around and ask what the benefits are, to ask what they get in return for hiring a consulting firm. These days, partly because of the recent economic downturn, but also because the technology fear-factor is lower, clients are looking to drive out value from the systems they have, rather than purchase new systems. Similarly, I think we'll see clients focusing even more on their core competencies. Where they are considering new technology purposes, the objective will be to ensure that their business functions can be integrated, not simply within their organisation, but between themselves and potential partners. Technology will, in effect, become the critical factor that enables organisations to focus on their core business. For years now, they've been questioning the rationale for – say – having an in-house accounting department, but the logistics of outsourcing it were prohibitively complex. The technology now exists which makes these kind of relationships viable, both technically and commercially. And the model that involves spinning-out functions such as accounting has given us an apparently effective vehicle for allowing companies to shed their non-core activities in a managed way.

It's now clear that you have to think about strategy and technology in tandem. And, if you accept this point, then one of two scenarios follows: either the technology has to become far more modular – 'plug-and-play' packages, to fit in with a customised strategy; or the reverse, that strategy has to become 'plug-and-play', around customised technology. The first of these models is where we have expected the market to go, a couple of years ago, but all it takes is for one large technology provider to start bundling strategy consultancy in with its hardware or software products, and to roll the fees up into the licence agreement, to change the balance of power significantly. Similarly, what would happen if an outsourcing company got its act together and built implementation into its service offering? How much work would really be left in the standalone consulting market?

As a result of these pressures, you'll see different configurations of consulting firms emerge in the future. And I'm not sure that consulting firms taking on the role of venture capitalists is the right way to go about doing this. Successful reconfigurations will occur where individual consultancies recognise and build on their core competencies, and I'm not at all convinced that those of a typical firm will position it well in the venture capital market. There's a very different kind of culture involved, for example. It's a relationship that may work between consulting firms and software companies, where the former can play the role of a branded-distribution channel rather than a straightforward investor, but the arguments for a relationship between a consulting company and – say – an oil company are far less compelling.

At the end of the day, consulting is one of two things: it can be a source of high-quality intellectual capital, or a supply of bodies – additional labour during periods of peak activity. I'd argue that some of the large mergers that are being talked about are primarily based on the second of these premises – scale therefore matters. That doesn't sit well with clients' desire for the former, something that, in many cases, translates into a firm's ability to field – and be seen as capable of fielding – a smaller number of world-class specialists. I think one of the important factors in the next few years will be the extent to which the very large firms can go through a managed process of spinning-out separate, more specialist companies, each with their own, distinctive brand. Some firms, I'm sure, will be able to control the process so that it creates additional value, but you can't help thinking that others will find themselves in the middle of an 'unmanaged' process, in which groups of consultants unilaterally spin-out to create their own companies.

To survive, let alone thrive, in the future, consulting firms are going to have to redefine what business they're in – they're going to have to re-invent themselves. If they're going to provide the highly specialised input their clients are increasingly demanding, and protect their services from being absorbed into the large-scale technology companies, then they're going to have to be focused much more around the process of identifying and exploiting their clients underused intellectual property. ’

15

Association of Management Consulting Firms

Betsy Kovacs

AMCF represents leading management consulting firms worldwide. Its membership is diverse: large and small firms, traditional management consultants as well as providers of professional services, generalists and specialists, single-office firms along with multinational organisations. Founded in 1929 as ACME (Association of Management Consulting Engineers), the AMCF remains in the forefront of promoting excellence and integrity in the profession.

Just as consultants help clients manage change within their industries, AMCF helps its members cope with the rapid changes affecting their practices today. With offices in New York and Brussels, it serves as a resource for information on the management of a consulting practice. It provides a forum for the exchange of ideas, helping consultants to better understand developments within the profession and to capitalise on new opportunities.

AMCF also serves as the voice of the industry on major issues, representing the profession before government and regulatory bodies, working to improve standards and practices and enabling firms to work smarter.

Elizabeth Ann (Betsy) Kovacs is president and chief executive officer of the Association of Management Consulting Firms (AMCF). She is a professional association executive, beginning her association management career as head of the Association for Advancement of Behaviour Therapy; led in the establishment of, and served as first chief executive officer of, the Society for Behavioural Medicine and for 13 years was executive vice president and chief staff officer for the Public Relations Society of America. Prior to joining AMCF, she was programme director for the International AIDS Vaccine Initiative.

Kovacs has an MAT from Yale University and an MPH from

Columbia University. She received the CAE (certified association executive) designation from the American Society of Association Executives, and has served on the ASAE and ASAE Foundation boards. She is also a Fellow of ASAE, a member of the Board of Directors of the Women's Commission for Refugee Women and Children of the International Refugee Committee and a member of the Women's Foreign Policy Association.

‘From what we hear from our member firm representatives, I think it's clear that we're still in the ‘pontoon-building’ phase of the application of web-based technologies – the cusp of a continuing revolution: ‘e-business’ isn't dead and done – it's just that it's becoming fully integrated into the fabric of business. We can't today imagine what it must have been like to run a business without access to a telephone: the same is becoming true for e-business. For clients, the problem has been rather like travelling to a new place: there's just so much to see and do, with limited resources, that it's often hard to decide what to focus on.

And I think this ‘revolution’ has produced – and will continue to produce – massive changes in the consulting industry, even though the spike in fee revenue (also inflated by Y2K-related income) has levelled off. Looking forward to how the AMCF believes these changes will pan out in the future, we believe that there's going to be a period of continued consolidation. In terms of market structure, we expect to see a continuing polarisation of the industry between the very large and the very small firms, with alliances between the two types of firm continuing to play a role. Mid-sized firms, we believe, may suffer from the twin pressures of, on the one hand, being unable to meet the breadth and depth of skills demanded by clients and, on the other, being too big to be a boutique specialist in just one area.

At the same time, there'll be a further broadening of what we mean by ‘consultancy’, and a blurring of boundaries between industries and professions. This will be caused by consulting firms adding new services to their existing portfolio, particularly in outsourcing, and offering a broader array of services such as law, as well as competition from non-traditional sources such as non-consulting organisations. Why would a parcel distribution company, like FedEx, launch a consulting service? Because it realises that it's delivering ‘solutions’ as much as parcels. You no longer go to your travel agent simply to purchase a ticket, but to have someone who can provide a ‘solution’, to offer the least expensive, most effective travel arrangement. This reintermediation is a far cry from what we expected from an intermediary five years ago.

That's changing the client-consultant relationship: we see clients being far more selective in terms of who they want to work with. Increasingly, we're also seeing them move towards having preferred-supplier lists of pre-qualified consulting firms with whom they have a long-term relationship. Increasingly, we hear about fees being linked to outcomes.

In this environment, the question of a firm's ownership will, we believe continue to be critical. Many firms have gone through IPOs forcing others to consider doing so. Many continue to grapple with this issue, and there's a whole array of models emerging as a result. Should the whole firm go public, or just part of it? Do you go for an IPO but hand over a lot of shares to your employees in the process, so the firm becomes partly owned by them? Part of the problem is that there won't be a single answer: different firms have different objectives, and these may well require different ownership models. One suit won't fit all. The idea of consultants taking equity stakes in their clients confuses the picture further. Clearly, one has to be concerned about the extent to which, in such circumstances, firms can maintain the objectivity and independence for which they have been historically valued. It also raises complex questions over firms' potential risks and liabilities. The current slowdown in the economy and the effects of the demise of the dot.coms appears to be making firms more cautious about investing in clients.

In five years' time, the consulting industry will look very different. It's possible that the only component that will remain constant will be strategy consulting: there'll always be someone at the helm of the organisation who wants an outside perspective, and I can't see that changing significantly in the future. But, if you total up the other likely changes – the polarisation of the market between boutique specialists and genuinely global firms; the continuing breakdown of barriers between countries with globalisation; the continuing inter-relationship of consultancy and technology; new sources of competition; the boundaries between firms dissolving as more organisations become linked to each other via alliances and affiliations – the changes will be great. According to surveys, fewer than 25 per cent of families in the United States could be classed as 'nuclear': far more complex family structures – extended, interwoven – are emerging. The same is becoming true of business: organisations – and that includes consulting firms – are likely to increasingly be a loose-knit fabric of individuals.

And that structure will mirror a growing recognition of the importance of the human factor in technologies. 'Show me the steak', is what clients are saying: 'help me drive the profits out of my systems and processes'. You can't do that without taking the human angle into account. We used to say that the human angle was the least predictable component of business.

However, now it appears that the unpredictability of people can be counted on: it's the new technologies that are the least predictable. The impact of the new technologies on people will be the focus of much of our consulting work. We believe this opens up new emphases in the consulting engagement, but may be a more difficult concept to sell to clients: it's much easier to sell machinery than it is motivation. ’

16

Bain & Company

John Donahoe

Bain & Company is one of the world's leading global business consulting firms, serving clients across six continents. It was founded in 1973 on the principle that consultants must measure their success in terms of their clients' financial results. Bain's clients have outperformed the stockmarket 3 to 1. With 2,800 employees, headquarters in Boston and 27 offices in all major cities throughout the world, Bain has worked with over 2,000 major multinational and other corporations from every economic sector, in every region of the world.

John Donahoe is Bain & Company's Worldwide Managing Director. He is responsible for overseeing the firm's 26 offices and over 2800 employees around the world. Donahoe joined the firm in 1982.

Donahoe's client work has focused primarily on major corporate transformations. He has served clients in the telecommunications, airlines, aerospace and financial services industries. Several of these client relationships encompassed a wide range of activities including corporate and business unit strategy and significant implementation in change management support. Donahoe has particular interest in customer loyalty and retention.

In addition to his client work Donahoe has held a variety of management roles and positions within Bain. He served as Head of the San Francisco office for seven years and has been a member of the firm's operating and nominating committees. He was elected Bain's Worldwide Managing Director in the fall of 1999.

Prior to joining Bain, Donahoe worked for the Rolm Corporation and Salomon Brothers. He earned an MBA from Stanford Graduate School of Business where he was an Arjay Scholar. Donahoe is a graduate of Dartmouth College where he received a Bachelor of Arts with high distinction, *magna cum laude*, in Economics, and was elected Phi Beta Kappa.

Donahoe serves on the Board of Directors of the Bridgespan Group, an innovative non-profit firm launched by Bain to bring strategic consulting capability to the non-profit sector, eVolution Global Partners, and Sacred Heart Schools in Menlo Park California.

❛In my view, many of new entrants we have seen enter consultancy since 1998 will have only a moderate long-term impact on the industry. Every industry goes through cycles of growth and consolidation – it's a healthy, Darwinian process from which the survivors will emerge the stronger. At the peaks of these cycles, you inevitably see new entrants and increased experimentation, and that's exactly what has been happening in the consulting industry over the last couple of years. We may now be entering a period of economic turbulence and uncertainty, and we will see a period of rationalisation and consolidation.

Three years ago we carried out an analysis about which companies emerged as winners during periods such as these. The findings were very interesting and concluded that it's periods of turbulence – not, as one might suppose, the peaks of the economic cycle – that produce the greatest movement in sustainable competitive positioning, and that the strong firms have the potential to emerge even stronger as a result. Those who did emerge strengthened had three things in common: first, they focused ruthlessly on their core business; second, they were prudent in terms of managing their own organisations and costs so that they did not have to be reactive later on and, finally, they took advantage of their relative financial strength to invest selectively for the future, either by moving into niche market adjacencies or by making focused acquisitions.

These are precisely the same strategies we've applied at Bain. We've stayed – and will continue to stay – true to our core values of helping clients develop customised, proprietary strategies which deliver bottom-line results. We've consistently said that a website is not a strategy, and that 'e' belongs inside strategy.

Rather than trying to diversify, we've used the last couple of years to strengthen our core ability to deliver value to our clients. Our starting point has been – and will continue to be – to stay obsessively focused on our clients' needs and how can we help them get improved results. We constantly ask them what capabilities do we need to help them do this? What kind of people and products? What kind of knowledge? It's a simple paradigm: we put our clients at the centre and build our business around them.

If you think about those words – 'customised, proprietary strategies' – they are even more important today than they were ten years ago. A decade ago, we were working in an environment of clear-cut industry boundaries. The strategies of the players within each sector were broadly similar: the winners were those who executed better than the rest. But, as the boundaries between industries collapse, no two businesses can define their strategy in the same way.

Like our clients, we have to be absolutely clear about where we have world-class capabilities, and where we don't: we're world-class at developing a proprietary strategy for a client, then helping to design the implementation blueprint, at tying the blueprint to organisational metrics that will drive its execution, and at initiating the first steps a business takes towards implementation, but there comes a point in the process at which other companies can provide a more cost-effective service – implementing software packages, for example. It's to both our clients' and our own advantage to do this, because world-class companies want to work with world-class suppliers, and it's difficult to be world-class if you're trying to offer everything – strategy, operations and technology.

Have the last few years challenged that way of thinking? Yes and no. For instance, do I think that technology is increasingly an integral part of strategy? Yes. Do I believe strategy and technology have become so profoundly inseparable that it makes sense for a business to hire strategy consultants from its hardware or software suppliers? If you look at high-end strategy – our market – I think the answer is no.

It is interesting because if you take the top ten technology companies in the world, we've worked with many of them. These companies know more than anyone about technology, but they still have strategic issues that they want help with. The fundamental question for a business is how it creates and continues to offer value to its customers – technology can enhance this value, but it cannot become a substitute for it. Technology is an enabling tool. Look at how you can improve productivity for example; technology obviously plays an important role here for clients, just as it does in our own business. But does that mean we need to change our recruitment profile in order to hire more technical specialists? What we look for at Bain are people with a high level of intelligence, who are effective communicators, but who can also think in practical terms. Today, any person who fits this profile is automatically going to have a much higher level of IT knowledge than they would have had, say, ten years ago. We now have a generation of chief executives who are much more comfortable with technology than their equivalents would have been a few years ago: it's no longer a black box to them where the benefits have to be accepted on trust.

In fact, we've used exactly the same logic with respect to the relationship between strategy and technology suppliers: we're clear about where we're world-class and we aren't going to be tempted to overstep the line we've drawn for ourselves. That's also one of the reasons why we formed BainNet – our alliance partnership of technology companies, each of whom is world-class in its own specialist niche: we know where we fit, and we know where they fit. It enhances Bain's core capability of making our clients more valuable by guiding them beyond strategy and through IT execution. And we can continue to be completely objective on technology-related decisions, which we believe clients will increasingly value.

We take the same view about the use of technology within our own business as we do with our clients: it's there to improve the effectiveness of our core capabilities, not replace them. Thus, we put a lot of emphasis on leveraging our knowledge with clients, currently via intranets on which we can not only put up information relating to an engagement in progress, but update the data and analysis even after the end of the engagement. Whereas traditionally we may have gone into a client with a series of slides summarising our findings, now we can put that information on the Intranet and keep it up-to-date so that the client continues to reference it.

Similarly, we use technology to help us allocate our resources as effectively as possible, but I can't ever see our staffing functions being replaced by technology. There are too many human components to them: it takes judgement and personal knowledge of those involved to place consultants in engagements, something even the most expert of expert systems is unlikely to match.

What I've said so far has focused on what Bain is doing in order to emerge stronger from the current period of economic turbulence. But we're also pursuing the third strategy I mentioned – using our position of comparative strength to make focused investments – investments in acquiring new talent, in strengthening our position in certain geographies and in improving our service to our clients.

We've done a considerable amount of research on the way in which sustainable success comes from driving the profits out of the core of your business: maybe we'll be proved wrong in the future, but, if we are wrong, then it won't be because we didn't have a point of view!

And going forward? There's always going to be a need for high-end strategy and implementation support. If anything, the job of the chief executive is getting lonelier and the pressure to produce results is getting greater. In an environment where the boundaries are multiplying, the resulting complexity is more than any one chief executive can keep a grip on. In our segment of the consulting industry, you have to be completely focused on delivering results for clients – everything else follows from this – and you have to be completely objective – clients need to be sure that the advice you give them is not motivated by the desire to sell other services at a later stage. I think for firms like Bain, the partnership model will still be the best way of doing business, as it provides the most effective mechanism we know for ensuring that we have the commitment of our people and for allowing us to take a long-term view, rather than worry about how investors might see our performance in the short run. No firm has broken into the high-end strategy segment of the industry since Bain was founded: where new firms have emerged they've ended up being acquired by players in other segments, and I don't think that will change. ’

17

The Boston Consulting Group

Philip Evans

The Boston Consulting Group (BCG) is a general management consulting firm widely regarded as the global leader in business strategy. For 36 years, BCG has worked with companies in every major industry and global market to develop and implement strategies for competitive success. Founded in Boston in 1963, BCG now operates in 32 countries and 47 cities around the world.

BCG's business is organized around industries and topics that define the strategic management imperatives facing global businesses today. They include: branding, consumer goods and retailing, corporate development, deconstruction, electronic commerce, energy and utilities, financial services, globalization, health care, high technology, industrial goods, information technology, and organizational and operational effectiveness.

Philip Evans is a pioneer in thinking strategically about the central business challenge of the new decade: the seismic confrontation between the old economy and the new economics of information. Leaders of incumbent businesses need to abandon their traditional assumptions about information channels, and the hierarchies, organizational boundaries and power asymmetries that those channels have traditionally defined. Insurgents need to move beyond experimentation and growth for its own sake, to a hard-edged focus on competitive advantage. Evans's award-winning writings on the 'deconstruction' of traditional strategy provide the unifying principles that enable both groups to understand and master their future: a fusion of legacy assets with an insurgent mindset. His thinking lays the foundations not just for Internet business and electronic commerce, but for strategy, organization and the concept of the corporation itself in the coming decade.

Evans is a senior vice-president with the Boston Consulting Group, and co-leader of BCG's practice focused on the new economics of information. He consults to CEOs of corporations in America and Europe in the consumer goods, media, high technology, and financial services industries. He is a frequent speaker at industry, corporate and academic conferences.

He was educated at Cambridge University, where he was admitted first in the entrance examinations, and graduated with Double First Class Honours in economics, obtaining the highest individual degree in the University and winning two University prizes. He was a Harkness Fellow in the Economics Department at Harvard and then obtained an MBA with honors from the Harvard Business School.

Evans is co-author of three *Harvard Business Review* articles, one of which, *Strategy and the New Economics of Information* won a McKinsey Prize, which is awarded annually for the best contributions to the *Review. Blown to Bits: How the New Economics of Information, Trasnsforms Strategy* (co-authored with BCG's Tom Wurster, published by the Harvard Business School Press) was the best selling book on the new economy in 2000, and has been translated into ten languages.

❛The consulting industry's currently going through a period of adjustment. The technology industry and instant millionaires of the dot.coms created enormous pressure on the demand side and from the middle of 1999 to the middle of 2000, the key challenge facing firms was how to manage this, especially as their own staff were leaving, attracted by the apparent wealth opportunities. For the high-end firms, like The Boston Consulting Group, this amounted to a substantial crisis, as it was the people working in these firms who were also the most employable elsewhere, and you saw a variety of responses to this – pay rises, venture capital funds (which I think were aimed much more at enhancing their image with potential recruits than at investing in outside ideas). At first, the market collapse in April 2000 looked like a blip, but by the fall of that year it was obvious that the boom was over: suddenly recruitment and retention were not an issue – the real problem was excess capacity.

The industry has been through trade cycles before, and, from that perspective, the implications of this downturn aren't material in the long-term. We'll see the strong players becoming stronger, and the less strong being subsumed. But that analysis belies the more profound, philosophical lessons of the last two years. In the first place, I think consulting firms had forgotten about the business cycle: like their clients, they believed the myth that it was possible to go on growing forever. They're over-steering the boat: recruiting massively during the peaks of demand, shedding them during the troughs. A useful moral that the managers of consulting firms should take away is the need to steer to a straight heading, rather than veering off with every individual current you come across – even if you have to leave some opportunities on the table as a result. Recent history has also shown us the extent to which capital markets are capable of 'bubbling up' business, and that leads to all sorts of nonsense. We have to remember that investors are like lemmings: it may be rational to be the first to throw yourself off a cliff, but it creates a self-fulfilling prophecy when everyone else follows you. Consultants should be less susceptible than clients and investors to passing management fads: they ought to be smarter and more strategic. The trouble is that it's quite rational behaviour to try and call the market – in this case, to pick up an emerging idea and promote it ahead of your competitors, or drop an idea before everyone else does. So the temptation exists for every firm to promote an emergent idea. The trouble is that no one's able to do it on a sustained basis: calling the market once or twice is just luck. There may be a small number of very wealthy people drinking mint juleps in Florida who've made their money by doing this consistently, but I doubt it. And for consulting firms, it's a slippery slope in practice: they'll think that picking one winner means they can do it again and again.

But the boom-and-bust economics we've observed over the last few years doesn't deny the significance of what's happening. Just because we now know that all those kids in garages aren't going to replace large corporations doesn't negate the fact that the pace of technological change is increasing. As the philosophers of the French Revolution noted, every revolution devours its own children – we saw that with the railroads. But, just because the revolutionaries are the earliest victims, doesn't mean that the revolution stops: the recent carnage shouldn't make us underestimate the significance of what's going on.

Indeed, the last few years are a testimony to how much we tend to overestimate the impact of short-term changes and underestimate the impact of long-term ones. Changes tend to be bigger and slower than we generally perceive them, and one of the dangers now is that we'll see a drift back to 'business as usual'. Our common analogy for change is a tidal wave: it's that which gives us strategic imperatives, such as the need to live on the edge. But perhaps a more appropriate analogy would be with the tectonic pressures that build up to cause earthquakes – that most change happens beneath the surface, only occasionally manifesting itself in cataclysmic shifts. This is just as threatening – if not more so – as the conventional tidal wave analogy, as the changes are more insidious, less easy to predict from the surface. I think that the changes that will produce a second internet generation are already happening and are largely going unrecognised. We've seen major upheaval in the music industry as the result of being able to stream digitised music directly to end-users: what's going to happen when we start streaming digitised television or video? Will today's television companies still exist in ten years time? Will companies that we think of as 'new economy', in fact be the first victims of the next revolution? As companies wake up to the rapidly changing economics of data compression, to the fact that consumers will be able to watch what they want whenever they want to and zap any advertisements in the way, they're going to see – for instance – that broadcasting is dead. Another example would be car dealerships – an intermediary which we predicted would be put out of business by the Internet.[1]

The kind of strategy you help clients to develop in an earthquake zone is very different to those facing a tidal wave: you're much more concerned to shore up the existing organisation so that it can withstand unpredictable stresses, than to be continually innovative. It may sound old-fashioned, but I think this brings you back to think about core competencies, particularly in the context of the new technologies now emerging, and I think that applies as much to consulting firms as the clients they advise. In 1999, firms over-responded to the Internet and treated it as a tidal wave of change. Now, they're probably under-responding to the technology changes which are happening below the surface, and there's a real threat that they and their clients will fail to grasp the significance of them.

And how will these changes affect consulting firms themselves? I can certainly see some areas of the industry, particularly where a fairly mechanical template is applied to the consulting process (most obviously IT consulting), or where the level of pure advice is very high (tax consulting, for example) being disintermediated by online, expert systems. But the kind of strategy in which The Boston Consulting Group is involved is so heavily embedded in the dynamics of a relationship – mutual trust, a shared vocabulary, a community in a very rich sense of the word – that I don't think that technology will be much more than an enabler. You couldn't create this kind of relationship without being there on purpose.

I think you'll see a similar difference in the pressures facing these types of firm internally. At the more routine, standardised end of consulting, there'll probably be pressure to fragment, to break up the sum of the organisation as a means of increasing the value of the parts. But at the high end, the reverse will be true: firms will be able to increase their value by better integrating their component parts. However, I don't think the firms that break up will do so along their original fault-lines: rather as we've seen in other industries, they'll deconstruct themselves into different forms which cut across traditional industry boundaries. So far as consultancy is itself concerned, some of that deconstruction will challenge some of the most accepted dichotomies of the industry – the separation of strategy from organisational change, and competition *versus* collaboration. Traditionally distinct disciplines will merge to create new paradigms. Some firms – like The Boston Consulting Group – will, I believe, be able to straddle these merging and demerging markets, but there are many more who'll struggle in this environment: the revolution will consume more of its children. ’

[1] Philip Evans and Thomas Wurster, *Blown to Bits: How the Economics of Information Transforms Strategy* (Cambridge, MA: Harvard Business School Press, 2000).

18

Cap Gemini Ernst & Young

Chris Meyer

Cap Gemini Ernst & Young is one of the largest management and IT consulting firms in the world. The company offers management and IT consulting services, systems integration, and technology development, design and outsourcing capabilities on a global scale to help traditional businesses and 'dot companies' continue to implement growth strategies and leverage technology in the new economy. The organisation employs about 60 000 people worldwide.

Christopher Meyer is a Vice President at Cap Gemini Ernst & Young and the Director of its Centre for Business Innovation in Cambridge, Massachusetts. He is also co-author, with Stan Davis, of two forward-looking business books: *BLUR: The Speed of Change in the Connected Economy* and *Future Wealth*, which identifies how structural changes in the economy are affecting our understanding of risk and opportunity.

Prior to joining Cap Gemini Ernst & Young, Meyer was a Vice President at Mercer Management Consulting, where he founded and built the firm's practice in the information industries, comprising telecommunications, hardware, software, and information services and media. He led relationships with several of the firm's leading clients—some spanning ten years—helping them pioneer concepts of capability-based strategy, horizontal and process management and the future of business in the information economy. His group won awards for service excellence from AT&T and Texas Instruments.

Meyer holds a BA in both mathematics and economics from Brandeis University and a MBA with distinction from Harvard Business School. In addition, he held a University Predoctoral Fellowship in economics at the University of Pennsylvania.

He serves on the Board of Directors of the Bios Group and Icosystems and on the Board of Advisors of LaunchCyte and the Museum of Music.

The Centre of Business Innovation is a cross between a think tank and a research and development group. It has three missions – to differentiate the firm as a thought leader in the marketplace, to create new services (the Bios Group, for example, looks at the application of chaos theory to management), and to take new ideas to clients, in collaboration with the account handling teams.

What we're seeing is not so much the disappearance of e-business as its assimilation into every company: you could say that it's become second nature – more of an assumption than an innovation –with increasing connectivity between organisations, this becomes a universal competence. The focus on wireless is just the current step toward a 'global, mobile, always on' network. The next step will be to attach more sensors to the network. Today, we have put sensors in the smoke stacks of power stations to monitor constantly the sulphur dioxide emissions. Think how important this technology could be to healthcare: someone with a weak heart could not only have a defibrillator implanted, the device could call an ambulance instantly if it detected the need. The network will grow nerves: it will become conscious.

How will these trends change the consulting industry? I think they will undoubtedly create a push for greater innovation, especially in the big firms. With the ERP vendors continually trying to encode new capabilities into their software, consulting firms have to innovate in order to have something to offer. Moreover, it took the large firms way too long to respond to e.business as it became the new management bandwagon: we're already seeing that response time shrinking where mobile commerce is concerned, but there's still room for improvement. Clients notice if a firm is slow: it makes them less likely to use that firm when the next bandwagon comes along.

And those challenges will keep on coming: connection leads to information, and information leads to efficient markets. The whole world is starting to look more and more like the financial markets, with real-time information available to buyers and sellers. That means there'll be more explicit management of risk –a four-letter word in an industrial environment but which has positive value in a financial market. Every kind of business is going to have to become more comfortable with risk. Thus we've seen the explosive growth of weather-based derivatives in the past five years, as companies from agribusiness to ski resorts start acting on better information. We also need to be able to apply this approach to consultancy: if clients are putting firms under pressure to be quicker and more innovative, then they have to understand that neither party can bear all of the increased risk. Risk sharing between client and consultant will become far more prevalent.

The strategy consulting industry has largely developed in response to scarcity. During the First World War, that scarcity was machinery, and Taylorism was a response to that. In the 1950s and 60s, it was market share that was scarce: hence the emergence of The Boston Consulting Group's growth share matrix. In the 1970s and 80s, the problem – spurred on by competition from Japanese companies – was quality, and, as a result, operational consulting, focused on performance improvement, predominated. 'E-business' had a short and brutish life, but I think it demonstrated the importance of good business ideas and business model competition– and I'd argue that this is the scarce commodity around which the consulting industry will focus in the future.

Taking that a stage further, I believe that consulting firms can help their clients face three important trends. First, is the strategic imperative to adapt more rapidly in the face of an accelerating pace of change: the military speak of 'getting inside your enemy's operating cycle, in order to pre-empt what he will do next. Put this together with the rapid evolution of simulation technology, and we'll begin to see strategy formulation taking place in a software environment in which genetic algorithms are used to 'breed' multiple variants on a company's strategic options, all of which can then be tested 'in silico'. Second, there's what I would call the 'molecular economy'. This has two meanings. First, biotech and nanotech are today where semiconductors and software were in the 1970s; soon, manipulation of molecules will be as big an economy as manipulating bits. The other meaning is that we'll see management from the bottom up, not top down. The management 'molecule' is the individual. Third, the molecular view will lead to the emergence of a 'science of management' in which business people use models honed in the biological sciences to simulate and understand problems they face. Ten years from now, I predict that we'll be designing organisations based on complex, agent-based models rather than flip-charts and spreadsheet.

Faced with these three trends, the challenge for consulting firms is to stay ahead of whatever can be encoded into software and therefore shared inexpensively. There will always be new management problems to solve: a firm's success will be determined by its ability to segment these problems into those that require a genuinely innovative solution, and those which could be best solved using pre-existing, codified knowledge. There are several directions consultants will pursue. We'll see more variety in terms of the tools and techniques being proposed by firms. This diversification will be just one of the ways in which firms look to mitigate their risks; another is the type of experiments many firms have made in the last few years in terms of investing in clients and changing their ownership structure. All enterprises, consultants included, will also have to adapt to the idea of permeable boundaries: consultants often talk about the conceptual 'firewalls' protecting their organisations and their intellectual assets, but a better analogy going forward would be with an immune system – you accept that you will be threatened with infection from time to time, but the key is to prepare your body to defend itself, not to stay indoors. Consulting firms in the future are going to be faced with all kinds of situations where they have less control they are accustomed to. Consulting engagements used to be like the Saturn project – one team with one objective: today, they're more like the International Space Station. It's going to take considerable maturity and openness to be able to handle this way of working.

Of course, all of this envisages that the basic model underlying the consulting industry remains largely unchanged. Is there anything that could revolutionise the consulting industry? The big threat we see is disintermediation: in fact, we think it's a sufficiently significant threat that we're trying to do something about it. If you put together several trends – the greater availability of information, the rise of the 'free agent' worker, the role of talent agents – then the traditional consulting model could find itself under a lot of pressure, as intellectual capital ends up in the hands of the buyer, not the seller. What we don't want to happen in CGE&Y's case, is that changes like these force us to act in an unconsidered manner: we'd rather act now to explore alternative models and, if necessary, look at paths by which we could migrate to them. In conventional consulting, the firm has employed the consultant and taken responsibility for the quality of his or her work. Sometimes – primarily in body-shopping – the client has taken over the responsibility, although the consultant has remained the firm's employee. In 1999, we launched Netstrike, a company that matched the qualifications of highly talented individuals who, for a variety of reasons, chose not to have permanent, full-time employment, with resource gaps in Fortune 1000 companies. In this model, we continued to have responsibility for quality, although we didn't directly employ those involved. We think there's an opportunity for a company that brings together these different relationships and which takes 'equity' in the individuals it places on projects with clients. In return we would invest in these individuals' development. But I don't think that means that the firm itself will have no role: the objective of the firm has to be to build critical mass, to provide the infrastructure and connections that will enable it to claim that it can help individuals make the most of themselves. Overall, we think this is going to be a real opportunity for both clients and colleagues. Fundamentally, I think it is wrong to see the firm as an overhead, it is the infrastructure that allows the individual to achieve economies of scale and scope. Chandler talked about structure following strategy, but I think in the future the relationship between these two is going to be more like the two strands in a double-helix, constantly intertwined: strategic choices will be both constrained and created by existing capabilities. Indeed, the co-evolution of strategy and organisational capabilities is one of the reasons why clients have been looking to consulting firms to help implement solutions, not just develop them in theory. Focusing on the scarce resource of the future – intellectual capital – and finding innovative ways in which it can be made to work for organisations will become the core mission of the consulting firm. ’

19

Deloitte Consulting

Stephen Sprinkle

Deloitte Consulting is one of the world's leading consulting firms, providing services in all aspects of enterprise transformation, from strategy and process to information technology and change management. The firm's professionals help the world's leading enterprises to create, reinvent and defend their business models by guiding them through the complexities of the evolving digital economy. Deloitte Consulting is part of Deloitte Touche Tohmatsu, one of the world's leading professional services firms, providing world-class consulting, assurance and advisory, and tax services through nearly 90 000 people in over 130 countries to nearly one-fifth of the world's largest companies, public institutions and successful fast-growing companies.

Stephen Sprinkle is a member of Board of Directors of Deloitte Touche Tohmatsu and Deloitte Consulting; he is also a director of Deloitte Ventures, a $500 m fund used to make synergistic investments in technology-based enterprises. and Telispark, a wireless computing software company.

As the Global Director for Strategy, Innovation and Eminence within Deloitte Consulting, Sprinkle's responsibilities include: the development of strategies and tactics to achieve the firm's strategic objectives; the identification of innovative services and approaches both to serving clients and to operating Deloitte's own business; research and development; and marketing. He was previously its Managing Director of Service Lines and Marketing, where he was responsible for Deloitte Consulting activity in service lines, marketing, knowledge and technology services, acquisitions, and alliances.

Sprinkle has an MBA in Finance from Adelphi University and attended The State University of New York at Stony Brook, from where he has a BS degree in Computer Science, Economics, and Applied Mathematics (where he was the first student in history of the University to complete three undergraduate majors).

‘The e-consultants are an exaggerated instance of something that has happened repeatedly in the consulting industry. With each new generation of managers, and each disruptive management idea, there's a period of time during which new consultancies spring up and grow very rapidly – you just have to look at what happened at the height of interest in shareholder value or client server technology to see this. The only difference, in the case of e-business, is that this cycle was exaggerated by the amount of capital available and this meant that many ideas and companies, which would not normally have gone beyond the business planning stage, found willing investors. In fact, the e-consulting sector grew too quickly for its own good, with firms being forced to deal with management issues in a matter of weeks that a firm growing at a 'conventional' rate would have had months, if not years to resolve before they became critical.

Going forward, I think there are four challenges for firms that continue to work in the e-business 'space'. First, they need to have the maturity to move with the market, as client needs change. Some of the firms that started out with a business-to-consumer focus found it very difficult to re-position themselves as clients' interests shifted. Second, a maturing market means a more sophisticated client base which recognises that generic solutions have little value to add. The onus will therefore fall on consulting firms to customise their solutions. But how do you do that without incurring a much higher level of costs? The effective management of knowledge will, I think, be key to being able to do this. Third, the new generation of e-consultancies will need to build global operations if they're going to secure work with the large multinational clients who typically form the bedrock of any sustainable consulting organisation. There's no way round this – and it's not easy: it means restructuring, moving resources to where demand is, and being able to integrate the abilities of multinational teams. Such clients – and this is the fourth challenge – also demand a high level of interaction with their consultants: as a firm, you need to have mature client handling processes and skills in order to be able to do this effectively and profitably. Looking at these new firms, I'd say that many of them placed too much emphasis on speed of delivery and creativity, and not enough on quality and the financial value of their work to clients.

I think clients panicked for a while – I think they believed they were doomed, and that that shook many of them into action. The key impact, I believe – and this wasn't something that was particularly noticeable at the time – has been in the way in which organisations have started to look at themselves as a portfolio of relationships – with their customers, suppliers, and so on. This had made them look more closely at how they run their core business without also having to run all those other processes which, while important, are not core. We're already seeing the results of this as organisations begin to build brands around that core and outsource their extraneous activities to 'wholesale' companies capable of delivering them more efficiently.

Something of this structure is also emerging in the consulting industry itself, where alliances are being formed that bring together branded players, who take primary responsibility for client relationship management, and specialist firms capable of providing in-depth expertise where required. At the same time, it's difficult to see how far this could go in practice: bricks and mortar companies have an incentive to make it happen because they're so capital-intensive, and that's clearly less of an issue for consulting firms. Moreover, the consulting industry has found it hard to balance heterogeneity and homogeneity: there's a lot of value in being able to provide clients with a common management approach, and that's difficult to maintain if you're trying to integrate a whole raft of organisations and individuals. I suspect that these factors mean that the model of a consulting firm that brings skills and processes together, rather than outsources them, will continue to predominate. And the plethora of firms that have come into existence since the late 1990s means that consolidation over the next few years has to be inevitable.

So far as technology-related consulting is concerned, I don't think this means a return to the kind of industry we had in the mid-1990s, which was dominated by large-scale ERP projects, mostly delivered by a small number of large consulting firms. Like many people, I'm personally uncomfortable with the idea of combined consulting, hardware and software companies because the temptation to be self-interested and to use the consulting practice to recommend the company's propriety technology will always be there.

Where I would have thought there is room for consolidation is in the strategy sector, even though this is the sector that, historically, has been least susceptible to restructuring of this type. The pressure for change is coming from investment banks who are increasingly offering strategy consultancy for free, as a way of inducing a transaction from which they can earn their fees.

Looking back on the impact of the last couple of years, I'd argue that e-business will have less impact on the consulting industry than ERP or even BPR – it's just that it received far more media attention. The idea of online consulting hasn't taken off and, although it's theoretically possible to provide advice remotely and there has been some small-scale experimentation, the idea that you can actually influence a client towards a particular course of action is as yet unproved. However, in the future it may be the case that some aspects of consulting are provided electronically – remote software development is the most obvious example, or tax consultancy, where the questions are specific and largely data-driven. While being only a subset of the consulting market as a whole, the first of these especially is not insignificant. This is somewhere where the alliances between 'branded' and 'wholesale' companies to which I referred earlier will I think have an impact on the consulting industry: in order to be able to deliver cost-competitive services, the 'branded' consulting firm will need to have an alliance with a 'wholesale' software development company. ’

20

DiamondCluster

Adam Gutstein

DiamondCluster International, Inc. is a premier business strategy and technology solutions firm, delivering value to clients worldwide by developing and implementing innovative digital strategies that capitalize on the opportunities presented by new technologies. The firm has more than 1100 consultants serving Global 2000 clients in such industries as financial services, consumer and industrial products and services, hi-tech, telecommunications and energy, healthcare and insurance. Headquartered in Chicago, DiamondCluster also has offices in Barcelona, Boston, Dusseldorf, Lisbon, London, Madrid, Munich, New York, Paris, San Francisco and Sao Paulo.

Adam Gutstein is President, North America of DiamondCluster International, and a member of the firm's board of directors. He is responsible for leading all aspects of DiamondCluster's business across North America. He also serves on DiamondCluster's Global Executive Committee and Worldwide Operating Committee.

A consultant for more than 15 years, Gutstein serves as a counsellor to senior management on how technology is transforming competitive landscapes and traditional theories on competition. In addition to his management responsibilities, he routinely serves as a 'hands-on' consultant and counsellor to senior management as he continues to guide DiamondCluster teams on major assignments. He focuses on engagements that blend state-of-the-art business strategy with cutting edge technology solutions to create significant business value for clients.

Gutstein was a co-founder of Diamond Technology Partners when it was formed in 1994, and played a significant role in the combining of Diamond with Cluster Consulting in 2000. Earlier in his career, he served in a number of management posts with Technology Solutions Company and Andersen Consulting.

'Yes, I think the consulting industry has changed over the last few years, but I also think it's changed continually since its inception. What we've tried to do at DiamondCluster is respond to this by building a firm that is genuinely multi-disciplinary, because we believe that's what clients both want and need if they're to be at the cutting edge of ideas and disruptive technologies – and to take advantage of them in terms of business results. For us, the priority has been to extend our way of working on a global scale: as we worked with larger and more prestigious corporations, they were increasingly turning round and saying, 'we love the work you've done for us in North America, but we want you to be capable of doing it in Europe, or in Asia, or in South America'. Hence the merger with Cluster, 95 per cent of whose business was in Europe and Latin America, in contrast to Diamond, 95 per cent of whose business was in North America.

What are the factors I see driving change in the future? In the short term, I think we're going to be living in a very volatile economy: we, like everyone else, have been surprised by the suddenness of the current [2001] slow-down. But, while capital expenditure – IT for example – is way down, consumer expenditure seems to be holding up: clients are very uncertain about which way things will go, and that means that they're not buying as much consultancy as they were doing. Our immediate challenge is to adjust to this change in demand. We don't want to go down the route of some other firms, of getting rid of our excess capacity: instead, our partners have unanimously voted to take a pay cut and we have developed a series of innovative programmes designed to retain our people, our most important asset by far. But in the long run consultancy is still going to be a great business to be in. As long as you have the best people, the best clients and the best intellectual capital – and you can wrap all of that up in order to create and execute ideas for your client' s advantage – then you can't fail.

Of course, doing those things isn't simple. Most start-up firms are looking for short-term success: they're focused around a particular issue or technology, and that's what they do well. Most find it hard to push back the boundaries of their business beyond this and, as a result, new firms come and go all the time. The difference surrounding DiamondCluster's philosophy – and this is one of the things we believe really distinguishes us from the other firms that have been founded in the last few years – is that we're in this business for the long term. Our partners and our people come from all walks of life, attracted by the idea that, whatever their background – be it strategy, marketing, technology, or execution – they'll be treated equally. Our diversity is one of our greatest strengths: we have, for example, a much higher proportion of women and minorities in senior consulting positions than most comparable firms. There are more than 50 nationalities represented in the people of DiamondCluster. Although lots of companies are trying to emulate IBM's model of integrating consulting services and hardware and software solutions, we don't see it as being that important – even though we've been approached by numerous potential partners. We do have an alliance programme; and while alliances between consulting firms and technologies vendors can supply both parties with a degree of comfort and an ability to manoeuvre on price, we believe that in the long run the only winning strategies are those that balance the needs of our people, clients, and our investors.

We've tried to find a more effective way of balancing the potentially conflicting needs of clients and shareholders by being what we think of as a public partnership model, in which we use the financial markets to raise capital, but operate internally as a partnership. Take for example our vote for a pay cut when the economy slowed in 2001: there's nothing in our by-laws that said we have to do this – and generally we don't do it on operational issues – but we did it then because we wanted to make everyone feel part of a partnership, that it was their decision as much as management's. In effect, we're trying to combine the best of public and private ownership structures. As a result, our rate of turnover is unusually low, which is a big part of both growth and quality.

Like other consulting firms, we've used the opportunity of the last couple of years to invest in clients and other ventures. On balance, I think we've done pretty well, but I'm not convinced that the trials and tribulations of involvement are worth it in the long term. If we're honest, I'd say that this is something consulting firms aren't especially skilled at, and, if – as we are – you're publicly owned, then managing the process externally, as well as internally, is hard. Clients certainly like it, and we're being increasingly asked to contribute to projects with which we're involved, but we've taken the view that we shouldn't be the principal investor. Private equity players are very different from consultants – they're concerned about extracting value, whereas consultants work in the best interests of the client – and are focused on creating value. We do, however, believe in the model – consulting firms should be well-positioned to add value through equity-sharing arrangements. We're just not convinced that the industry has yet found the best way of executing it: that's going to take time to work out.

We looked at hundreds of potential partners before we found Cluster, and when we did it felt as if we were twins separated at birth. In fact, we only found them because we were trying to recruit someone they were also trying to recruit: when it looked as though we were going to lose out, we thought we'd better find out who the competition was , because they clearly shared our culture and values. And I actually think that's what will mark successful firms in the future: you only get a good reputation and great people if you have a strong sense of your core values. But people businesses are the hardest businesses to run, although in many ways they are the most rewarding. I sometimes say that if I could come back in another life, I'd like to have at least a few physical assets as well – give me a bit of machinery or something! ’

21
Digitas

Daniel Flamberg and Patrick Rona

Digitas helps companies use technology, data and marketing strategies to connect with their customers across multiple channels. Digitas combines capabilities in digital strategy, technology, creative and integrated marketing to enable Global 2000 and other blue-chip companies connect the right message to the right customer through the right channel at the right time.

The firm serves as strategic partner to industry leaders, with clients including American Express, AT&T, General Motors, Kingfisher, L.L. Bean, Morgan Stanley, Fleet Financial, Allstate Insurance, PepsiCo and Terra Lycos. Headquartered in Boston, Digitas employs more than 1900 people and has offices in New York, Chicago, San Francisco, Salt Lake City, Miami, Monterrey, London, Brussels, Paris and Hong Kong.

Daniel Flamberg is the Senior Vice President for Digitas Europe, and leads the company's marketing and business development effort in Europe. He also serves as Relationship Leader on several global accounts.

Flamberg joined Digitas in 2000 after five years as President for Relationship Marketing at Ammirati Puris Lintas and Lowe Lintas where his portfolio included responsibility for direct, interactive, retail, e-commerce and customer relationship marketing where his clients included Dell Computers, Ameritech, GMC Trucks, GM OnStar, LEGO Systems, Ortho-McNeil Pharmaceuticals, Novartis, UPS, RCA and Goldman Sachs.

During his 24-year marketing career, Flamberg has worked on both sides of the business. As a client, Danny worked as Executive Vice President and Chief Marketing Officer of CellularONE, Chief Marketing Officer of the Radio Advertising Bureau and Vice President for Advertising and Promotion of the NBC Television Network.

He earned an AB, an MA and a PhD in politics and economics at Columbia University.

❛ What we're seeing now is a quasi-Darwinian process in which the ventures that shouldn't have received funding over the last couple of years, are becoming extinct. Evolution, if you like, is working its magic. If we look back at the founding of the railroads in the early part of the nineteenth century, we can see exactly the same process: the vast majority of those founded in the 1830s went bust before the Civil War, for the same reasons that we see today – over-promotion, unrealistic expectations, logistical constraints. It's a very close analogy. And, today, we're seeing established corporations – organisations that, two years ago, we were being told were slow to innovate – adopting many of the concepts pioneered by dot.coms and being very confident about their ability to adapt – evolve – in the future.

I'd therefore argue that the last two years have not had any dramatic impact on the fundamentals of the client-consultant relationship. What we saw in 1998–2000 was a hiccup, in which tremendous amounts of market anxiety swept away normal budgetary constraints and in which consultants themselves were caught up in the hype. But I think we have seen – and will continue to see – the clarification of the desire among clients for combinations of specialist skills. One lesson the last two years has taught them, is of the need for a variety of perspectives, rather than a single, monolithic interpretation of events. They're also more aware of the different competencies of individual consulting firms, and are becoming clearer and more precise about how they want to dovetail these skills with those of their own organisations. I think this means that the idea of one-stop-shopping won't prove viable: clients don't believe that a single firm can do everything. 'That's not credible', they're saying. 'What do you really do?' It's a bit like a Christmas tree – underneath all those glittering trimmings, there's a solid tree – and that's want clients want to see – but some trees are so heavily decorated that it's not easy to look beneath the surface.

The challenge for consulting firms will be knowing which areas of specialisation to pick. I'd say that there are essentially three options: you can be a strategy firm, a creative firm, or a technical enabler, and the right option for one firm will not be the right option for another. If you walk through the door marked 'strategy', then you can be reasonably comfortable that your margin will be high – certainly higher than if you'd chosen one of the other two options. But there won't ever be a large number of strategy projects, and their average length will probably continue to decline – so you may be profitable, but you probably won't be large. By contrast, walk through the door marked 'technology', and you'll find plenty of work to do, but you may have problems keeping your margin.

History has already shown us that this is the type of work that is most vulnerable to commoditisation so most competition will therefore continue to be on price. Moreover, clients know that the tables have turned: a couple of years ago, firms could feel confident about turning work away – the level of demand was so high – but in today's market clients know that there's significant over-capacity in the industry and are going to take advantage of it. Being able to withstand at least a temporary lowering of fee rates is going to be one of the most important factors in determining a firm's success in the near future.

Something else that has changed on the client side is their desire for consultants to be more 'directive'. They want the consultant to have a point of view. 'We hired you', they're saying, 'because we thought you either knew the answer already or had a process by which you could work it out. What we don't want is a series of options.' And this is happening at all levels: even where a comparatively junior consultant goes to the client with some alternatives about, say, the design of a part of the client's web-site, they're getting a similar demand for definitive answers. Clients want us to be completely certain about what we do – and, by extension, what they do – in all parts of a project. This attitude is reinforced by a trend which we see as growing rapidly – that clients want us to have some sort of financial commitment to the success of an engagement: it's not just that we have to give them the right answer, but that we have to implement it as well. In particular, clients are increasingly looking to strike incentive deals which may have a significant future upside for the consulting firm in return for discounted fees in the early stages of the project. They're tying our compensation into long-term performance, while also being able to go back to their own organisations and say 'hey, look at this great deal I just got!'.

A concomitant to this is that clients are demanding much greater transparency in the consulting process. At Digitas, we've created a whole new team focusing on delivery management, which we try to keep separate from the client relationship management part of a project. By delivery management, I mean the nuts and bolts of resource allocation, status against budget, and so on. We trying to be completely open about who's doing what and how much it costs, and we identify and get sign-off for every possible variance to the agreed plan. Although the overhead for us is considerable, we're finding that this approach is yielding a significant dividend in terms of increased trust between ourselves and our clients. Many of us – me included – were initially very sceptical about whether this was the right strategy, and we still hate the administration it involves, but we're in no doubt that we've seen client relationships get stronger as a result.

Take both of these trends – being more directive and having a financial stake in a project – and I think it's inevitable that we'll be siding with our clients. If they want a neutral perspective, in the future, they'll hire a business school professor. It's testimony, I believe, to a more risk-averse business environment. And, equally inevitably, this raises questions of conflict of interest between clients. As a firm, Digitas does a considerable amount of work in the financial services sector, and this issue is a particularly sensitive one there at the moment. So far, we've been able to use geography to ensure there is no conflict: thus, we've run one project out of our New York office, another out of Boston, another in London – and that's ensured that the client teams are entirely separate. But, increasingly, our clients are asking us to work on a global basis, and we're simply not large enough to maintain discrete teams in each office: that works fine in New York, where we've hundreds of people, but we've fewer in London. Furthermore, it's not simply a question of keeping different interests separate: yes, there's clearly important company information that has to remain absolutely confidential, but there's an enormous upside to clients in this sector continuing to use us – even if we have or are working with their competitors – because of our depth of knowledge about the sector as a whole. As an industry, we have to balance our fiduciary responsibility to keep confidential information confidential, but the non-client-specific knowledge we've been able to build up is tremendously valuable. In Digitas' case, we're continuing to use physically separate teams, and we've set up a compliance committee and opened ourselves up for security audits. But I don't know if that's going to be a sufficient solution in the longer-term: it's a code, and I'm not sure we – or any consulting firm – have cracked it yet.

Having a stake in a client's business takes us close to the topic of venturing by consulting firms. I suspect the extent to which an individual firm pursues this strategy will be largely dependent on their experience over the last two years. In Digitas' case, we decided to take only a very limited investment in a small number of companies, and – with the benefit of hindsight – I don't think we made the best choices. Of the seven companies in which we invested, only one survived and that was eventually sold. We chose to invest 'soft dollars' – that is, services, rather than cash – which meant that we had only a small stake in the companies concerned, certainly not enough for us to control those companies' operations and performance. I think the lesson we've learned is that this is probably an all-or-nothing strategy: if you're going to take a stake in a company, than it has to be substantial enough for you to be able to influence its direction. More generally across the industry as a whole, I think people have been forced to recognise that there's a real distinction between a consultant and an entrepreneur. One of the underlying problems with consulting firms taking on the role of venture capitalists has been cultural: entrepreneurs tend to be much more focused and ruthless, whereas a good consultant is a team player, who builds consensus. Consultants are also better at applying their advice to other people – that is, clients – than they are to themselves.

Going forward, I think the next big market for consultancy will be in systems and channel integration: we're only at the very start of a process in which both consumers and businesses are going to want more information distributed via many more devices. There's undoubtedly going to be a shake-out among the software vendors, and we'll probably see them consolidate around two to three dominant survivors. Does that mean that the technology consulting market will look as it did in the early to mid 1990s, when it was concentrated around a small number of ERP players? No, I don't think so. The primary difference will come from clients, who have learnt the lesson about buying and implementing very large packages wholesale. In the future, I think we'll see a lot more in the way of incremental purchasing, with clients buying only one module at a time, implementing that relatively quickly, and then moving on to the next issue. As consultants, that has to make us think about how nimble we can be: it will be a question of having many smaller, more responsive teams, and we have to decide how we're going to make that work. Making a margin on a single large project is comparatively easier: an equivalent margin in this more fragmented environment raises all kinds of questions. Do we move people around the world much more than we do at present? How will we allocate resources from one project to another? We're going to have to develop new ways of working and organising ourselves if we're to continue to maximise our expertise and profitability.

This, in turn, has implications for the kind of people we hire. The best people are going to become even more valuable than ever, so we'll need to invest even more attention both to our recruitment process and the means by which, once recruited, we retain these people. We also have to be aware that every consultant is client-facing these days. It used to be the case that you could have some 'geeks' in your organisation – real experts, but not people you'd want to put in front of a client – but everyone today has some client contact, everyone embodies the brand. In the future, everyone in a firm will be involved with selling – there'll be no distinction between doing and selling, everything will depend on individuals' ability to foster long-term relationships. ’

Since joining Digitas in November 1999, Patrick Rona has been a leading member of the senior Financial Services team, and most recently served as the relationship manager for MSDW's Investment Banking Division. Rona was responsible for managing the relationship across three offices (New York, Boston and London) and helping IBD formulate and execute its Internet strategy, including the launch of over ten extranet sites and the development of a 50+ person web services department.

Prior to joining Digitas, Rona was a Group Director at Agency.com, where he oversaw a number of accounts including British Airways, Hewlett Packard, Kmart, and Unilever. Previously, Rona was VP/ International Business Development for FirstMark Holdings Inc., a privately held company that invested in several wireless communications ventures throughout Latin America. Rona has a BA from Washington University.

'I think we're now in one of those periods in the consulting market, when clients have brought a lot of the expertise they want in-house. They've become much more expert about their business and consulting requirements, and they want to see precisely where a firm is going to add value. The most important area in which their internal expertise is still under-developed is in managing multiple channels, the question of how a business can deliver value to customers – or even employees internally – via the different routes now available. And this is a skill-set that clients will continue to find hard to build in the future, as it runs counter to what remains their conventional way of working – in functional teams and business units. People tend to focus on one channel rather than all channels simultaneously. The challenge for consultants is to do what their clients cannot – to look at all the variables, all the emerging technologies, and assess how these are going to affect and be affected by the end user.

One thing we find ourselves doing is using cases studies much more – rather than just facts – as we're finding that many of the issues are cultural, not intellectual. Clients often see a multi-channel environment as essentially a technology challenge: What platform should we use? Which vendor will set the standard? But the question is much more about how you ensure that you have a consistent brand, not just in different parts of the world, but through all the possible points of customer contact. *De facto*, therefore, we find ourselves dealing with organisational issues as much as technology ones.

How involved does that mean we become in the client's organisation? I think the answer to that question depends very much on the bias of the individual client. Both extremes exist: the client that wants to outsource quite significant areas of their business and hand over day-to-day responsibility for the organisation to the service provider; and the client that wants to retain as much expertise in-house as possible. It's a choice that depends on the extent to which a client sees their business as proprietary: clearly, where ownership and confidentiality are strong characteristics, then they'll tend to use consultants to work on specific problems and be more reluctant to cede control to a third party.

For consultants, the key will be to be – and be seen to be – on the client's side – and implementation is an important part of this. It's one thing to have a great idea, but another matter completely to be able to provide, first, the detailed road map which a client requires in order to realise the idea and, second, the ability to help the client travel that road. It's been some time since consultants could survive on ideas alone, but the majority of established firms have tended to stop at the point where they have delivered the road-map. They've developed the idea and told the client how to implement it – but the implementation will be someone else's job. That's one of the things that has changed significantly since the advent of e-business: consulting firms need to be able to do, as well as advise. I think we'll see a lot more moves in which firms merge with or are acquired by a major software or hardware developer – as they, in effect, attempt to replicate the success that IBM has had with its global consulting services.

So what will the critical success factors be for consulting firms in the future? I strongly believe that the greatest value a consultant can bring is a different perspective, one that's built upon his or her depth of experience but which provides fresh insight into the situation of a given client. This is going to be particularly important in what I believe to be a huge opportunity that's emerging for the consulting industry in contextual marketing – the problem of getting the right message to the right person at the right time, using the right medium. Again, people tend to see this as a technology issue, but it's really about how you interact with the customer when and where they want to, not when and where you want to.

It therefore seems clear to me that the firms that succeed in the next few years will be those that are capable of combining these two facets: deep specialisation with creative thinking. To be able to do this both effectively and profitably will involve considerable challenges to consulting firms internally. Perhaps the most obvious of these will be in the way firms not only manage knowledge, but also package it internally and externally – how they combine not just the intellectual content of an idea but the practical know-how required to deliver it. There'll also be even more of an imperative to 'think globally, act locally' as we have to understand how technology impacts customers differently in different geographical markets, rather than assuming that a trend exhibited in one area will automatically be replicated in others. Cross-border and cross-channel working will also mean that we have to recruit people with a more diverse set of backgrounds, and find some way of blending their different skills into a workable organisation but without blurring any of the distinctions between them. One of the lessons we've learnt from e-business is how important teams are that integrate strategic, creative and technology skills – and this is going to be even more of a challenge going forwards as we strive to include ever greater heterogeneity. Open internal communications become paramount here: to survive, consulting firms are going to have to foster the exchange of ideas – within the firm, between the firm and its clients – far more proactively than the majority do at present. Indeed, this is something that is hard to do by directive. Instead, you need an organisational structure in which you can rotate people between different teams, while also maintaining their specialist skills through peer-group pressure.

These qualities will be important because they go right to the heart of the value that clients obtain from consultants. One thing I think we've all learnt from e-business is the importance on focusing on real value, not hype. But you can only do this if you have the right people and the kind of organisational structure which is designed to meet the challenges this will involve. ’

22

iFormation Group

David Pecaut

iFormation is a company created by the strategy consulting firm, The Boston Consulting Group, the technology venture capitalist, General Atlantic Partners, and the investment bank, Goldman Sachs, to carve new ventures out of traditional companies in partnership with the Global 2000. iFormation teams with industry leaders to acquire, develop and build new Internet and technology ventures that leverage the corporate partners' legacy assets. iFormation's international network and management generates value for leading companies by emphasising speed to market, core business development and deep technology expertise.

David Pecaut is the President of iFormation Group, a global company headquartered in New York. Created by The Boston Consulting Group, Goldman Sachs and General Atlantic Partners, iFormation carves new Internet and technology ventures out of Global 2000 companies' existing businesses and legacy assets.

As the leader of iFormation, Pecaut acts as both strategist and 'business architect'– creating new business models for the Internet space, bringing together prospective partners to build them and taking equity positions with the objective of creating sustainable value.

Prior to joining iFormation, Pecaut was founder and leader of The Boston Consulting Group's global electronic commerce practice. Under his guidance, BCG's e-commerce team grew to offer clients a full spectrum of e-commerce consulting assistance from solving specific problems to managing the rapid start-up of entire online businesses. A well-known speaker and business strategist, Pecaut has worked with companies and governments in North America, South America, Europe, Asia and Australia. He is a widely sought-after speaker and media commentator who has appeared on CNN, CNBC and CBS, and he has been featured or quoted widely in newspaper and magazine articles, ranging from the Wall Street Journal to Business Week.

Pecaut holds a Master's degree in philosophy from the University of Sussex and an AB magna cum laude from Harvard College.

'Two significant trends have come out of the last two years, and not just from e-business, as the origin of these trends is much broader. First, clients are demanding that their consultants ring new insight and ideas: it's not enough if the thinking the consultants bring is simply incremental. Second, there's the level of impact required: clients don't just want a report, they want the implementation of that report.

Put those trends together, and I believe that there'll be three on-going segments in the consulting industry. There'll be the high-end strategy consultancies – the likes of The Boston Consulting Group, Bain and McKinsey. These are firms that are investing very heavily in their recruitment process, in research and development, and in knowledge management and sharing – all of which mean that these firms will be able to field the type of in-depth, cross-function and cross-industry knowledge for which clients are prepared to pay premium fee rates. The competition here will be all about finding the right business model – one that enables the firm to invest and reap the rewards of that investment very effectively.

Next, there'll be a small number of big systems integration firms who become increasingly adept at large scale programme management – a service that already accounts for a substantial part of these firms' income. Clients, I believe, will increasingly come to rely on these firms simply to get things done. The challenge facing these firms will be commoditisation – something to which their more standardised, scalable services will be especially prone.

Finally, there'll be the boutique specialists, who'll be like honey bees, focused on very specific areas and taking specific ideas from firm to firm. These firms will have success in narrow, expertise-intensive consulting fields, such as product development and branding. But, as they grow, many will be acquired by the large systems integrators, as the latter seek to stay ahead of the process of commoditisation; only a minority will be able to reinvent themselves as the market evolves. Those that succeed among these smaller firms will probably be those that have a charismatic leader. The firms that will lose will be the large-scale, generalist consultancies who will be vulnerable to the same process of commoditisation that will affect the systems integrators, but will have less in the way of technical and programme management skills which will allow them to withstand it.

Another facet that will characterise – and protect – the large-scale systems integrators will be the partnerships they establish with technology companies. The symbiotic relationship Accenture has with Siebel is a good illustration of this – and I think this will become the model other consulting firms will attempt to replicate. Such partnerships also create an opportunity for the high-end strategy firms, who can differentiate themselves as honest brokers of technology, as they have no vested interest in a client's purchase decisions. The Boston Consulting Group, for example, has set itself up as an 'IT navigator', capable of providing objective advice to clients against the whole plethora of available options.

Commoditisation will have much less of an impact on the high-end strategic consultancies, as the good firms will always be moving ahead of market developments, abandoning services before they become standardised, let alone commoditised. Of course, this means that such firms are never going to grow to the size of the systems integrators: economically, they'll continue to be characterised by a much higher ratio of partners to consultants, because the level of innovative thinking required will be much higher. They'll foster this innovative thinking by staying close to the 'rock face' in terms of client work. As long as they can continue talking to CEOs about the kinds of things that keeps the latter 'awake at night', then they will be able to identify new areas of work. Ten years ago, it was often academics who were doing this kind of research, who were, in effect, closest to the rock face, but e-business demonstrated how hard academia finds it to keep up in a rapidly changing environment. I recently went to a major European conference on efficient consumer response (ECR) where there were half a dozen CEOs on the platform, and many other executives and consultants, but few academics. The research cycles of the latter just haven't been able to keep pace with market changes. By contrast, the strategy consultancies have been investing more and more heavily in research; and some – like BCG – have set up think tanks.

I can't see anything out there that could realistically interrupt the relationship between CEOs and strategy consultancies. If anything, I think the relationship is going to be stronger and broader: faced with increasing complexity, more and more CEOs are turning to trusted outside advisors because they don't feel they can confide in their own colleagues.

Will venturing by consulting firms change this? I actually believe there are three different models of venturing, each of which has distinct implications. First, there'll be those firms that won't get involved in this. Yes, they may sometimes accept equity in lieu of fees, but only when they feel pressure to do so, and usually they have some means of separating these – blind trusts, for instance – from their mainstream business. At the other extreme, you have firms that have plunged headlong into venturing with their own capital funds and here you have to ask whether these firms have either the people or the culture to make this work. Finally, you have organisations like iFormation Group that have been specifically set up to partner with clients, and which combine the necessary skill sets. iFormation is a unique arrangement. It was created by The Boston Consulting Group, General Atlantic Partners and Goldman Sachs, to carve new ventures out of traditional companies in partnership with the Global 2000. iFormation teams with industry leaders to acquire, develop and build new ventures that leverage the corporate partners' legacy assets. We're looking to do a select number of significant ventures that we think are going to be category-killers. eOne Global, which we created with First Data Corporation, is a leader in payment innovation: it identifies, develops, and operates emerging payment systems and related Internet and wireless technologies spanning the business, government and consumer markets. We expect eOne to do over $80 m in revenues in its first year.

Site59.com is another venture with which iFormation is involved. It's a fully automated travel site that takes up unused capacity, not just from airlines but also hotel chains and car rental companies to create instant holiday packages. And the suppliers love us because we are selling their highly perishable inventory. This kind of approach isn't dissimilar to the way in which venture capital firms have approached leveraged buy-outs in the past. What I think is distinctive is our ability to bring together a very effective group of partners to operationalise these ideas and make them work.

What will determine the success of individual consulting firms in the future? The biggest issue facing the consulting industry is the 'war for talent'. At the moment, with people leaving the dot.com sector, some firms feel the heat is off, but this remains an enormous problem over the long-term. Beyond this perennial and intractable problem of finding and keeping good people, I think there's also the challenge of staying relevant, or being able to create an impact. The boom of the last couple of years has lulled at least some firms into a false sense of security, into thinking that being able to field additional pairs of hands is enough. In the future it won't be – at least not if a firm wants to continue to have the impact at CEO level which is where most professionally satisfying relationships lie. And I see the hourly fee-based business model of consultancy coming under severe pressure, as clients demand increasingly substantial evidence of commitment. Consulting firms will need to apply some of their innovative thinking to themselves, and reinvent their own businesses to meet these new demands. ’

23

KPMG Consulting

Alan Buckle

KPMG Consulting is one of the world's leading management consultancies, specialising in business solutions integration. It employs over 20 000 people in 71 offices worldwide.

As a firm, it believes that there are three overriding forces at work in the business environment: global competition, increasing customer sophistication and the all-pervasive impact of internet protocol technology. Reflecting this vision, its activities are focused around four principal industry sectors (consumer and industrial markets; financial services; information, communication and entertainment; and public services) and four key service lines (customer management; supply chain management; improving workforce performance; and finance).

KPMG Consulting Inc was listed on Nasdaq in February 2001. It became the first major consulting and solutions integrator to move out of a partnership and into public ownership.

Alan Buckle has been the driving force behind KPMG Consulting Europe's rapid evolution into a business solutions integrator, restructuring the business to be closer to its markets, faster to respond and deliver, and better able to innovate. He became CEO of KPMG Consulting UK in 1998 and COO for Europe a year later. In these capacities he has been responsible for integrating the European business into the firm's global strategy and business model and for overseeing the European implementation of a series of strategic alliances with major industry players such as Cisco, Microsoft and Compaq.

‘The ‘pure-play’ e-consulting firms – even though they've largely come and gone – certainly scared the incumbents. Why? Partly because of the speed of change required, but also because they brought in new skill sets, especially on the creative and branding side, which we lacked. But, ultimately, these new entrants have taught us a lot about our own strengths.

I believe we're at the start of a period that will see the industrialisation of the consulting industry: firms are adopting a more corporate style; many have access to capital they wouldn't have had in the past. And I think that greater maturity, combined with the swift rise and demise of the e-consultancies, has given the industry a self-esteem it didn't have before. Think of all the jokes you've heard about consultants: the majority originated from within the profession. In effect, the e-consultancies helped precipitate a very necessary period of soul-searching, in which the existing firms were forced to evaluate what was wrong with the consulting model, and what was right, and how we can create value for clients in the future. They changed the way consulting firms think about themselves: two years ago we wouldn't be sitting down with investment banks having the kind of conversations we have today – about financing, competitors, alliances, HR issues and so on. We tended to think only of our immediate peer group, not our position within the changing structure of the business world.

We certainly see the consulting industry restructuring around the very large solutions integration firms, some of which will be closely allied with technology providers, some of which will be independent. There'll be large players in this latter sector – indeed, I think we'll see the current 6–7 players consolidate to two or maybe three, led by those firms who have access to capital. And one of two things could happen: the independents could be beaten by the scale and muscle of those firms allied with technology companies; or (and I think this is more likely) people will in the long term begin to query the rationale for bringing together a consulting company and a software or hardware company. While the financial backing of a hardware or software partner may be helpful in the short term, longer term the level of business synergy may be too little to justify staying together. For the small, specialist firms, I'd argue that the future is very bright, as long as they retain their focus. A big firm doesn't necessarily have to be beautiful, but a small firm does. The firms that are neither big nor beautiful – the mid-sized firms or the small firms that try to emulate the large ones – are the most vulnerable, liable to be squeezed by both the economies of scale of the larger firms, and the specialist expertise of the most focused.

I think the need for pure strategy advice will linger – there are still moments when an organisation, or more likely, a CEO, wants to go off and think and they're willing to pay premium fee rates to those organisations capable of helping them do this. But I think growth in the industry will come from delivering solutions and changing organisations at a rate faster than they would have been able to achieve single-handedly. The need for fast, effective solutions is driving consolidation of the industry. Few organisations can have the breadth and depth of talent to deliver large scale solutions. Major, global clients will increasingly look to fewer suppliers and expect long term relationships.

We have to understand why clients are doing this. When they're buying consultancy clients usually take three things into account: the existing relationship they have with a firm, the expected benefit from the solution delivered, and price. Between these three factors, it's relationship that is by far the most important: clients have to be able to trust you – and that includes trusting you to tell them what you can do and what you can't. Price is usually the last consideration: if you find yourself, as a consultancy, only competing on price, then you're in trouble. Greater client selectivity isn't a threat to the consulting industry – although it could be to some firms – but it does mean that a firm's ability to nurture and sustain its client relationships will become even more crucial to its survival and success.

By association, consulting services will become more tangible – more 'productised' – than they have been in the past. Part of this is a reaction to greater scrutiny by the capital markets than has been the case historically in this sector: when you find yourselves being compared by the capital markets to a 'traditional' company with physical products, you have to be very clear about what your assets – intellectual as well as physical – are.

But the onus here is really on the consulting industry to start educating the investment community to have a better understanding of the consulting model and the metrics that typically underpin it.

If you buy the idea of industry consolidation, if you want to emerge as one of the remaining, dominant players, then you have to be publicly-owned. The question isn't particularly one of routine investment; this has been handled by partnerships. Public ownership enables organisations to distribute capital efficiently amongst its employees in a fast-changing environment – the partnership structure isn't designed to do this. In addition, the publicly owned will lead the transactions which will inevitably accompany the industry consolidation.

Like any business that's maturing, there's a lot of unfinished work around the consulting industry. Globalisation is still high up the list. Clients are increasingly global; projects are increasingly global. At the moment, we've got two models, neither of which may be the solution. In the first model, you take a firm with a strong culture in its home country and you try and replicate this culture elsewhere: it's an approach that has worked well for US companies expanding into the UK, but may lack the respect for cultural diversity required to survive in different markets in the long run. The second model is much more flexible and diverse, and is built bottom-up from different national businesses and cultures. Here, the problem is that it's more difficult to get things done.

The successful management consultancy in the 21st century must therefore develop a business model and culture that helps it find the right balance between steadfast vision and organisational flexibility, as well as between depth of expertise and breadth of solutions portfolio, in an ever-changing landscape.

24

McKinsey & Company

Ron Farmer

McKinsey & Company is a management consulting firm that helps leading corporations and organizations make distinctive, lasting and substantial improvements in their performance. Over the past seven decades, the firm's primary objective has remained constant: to serve as an organization's most trusted external adviser on critical issues facing senior management. With approximately 7100 consultants deployed from 84 offices in 43 countries, McKinsey advises companies on strategic, operational, organizational and technological issues. It has extensive experience in all major industry sectors and primary functional areas as well as in-depth expertise in high-priority areas for today's business leaders, such as growth, globalization and the new economy.

Ron Farmer is a senior director with McKinsey & Company, now based in Toronto. In his over 20 years with McKinsey, he has served clients in North America, Europe, and Asia, helping them improve their performance through renewal, restructuring, and repositioning. His work has spanned a range of strategy, organization and technology challenges for industries including banking, telecommunications, retail, media, electric utilities, mining, steel, pharmaceuticals and automotive. Most recently, Farmer has been very active in serving financial institutions, principal investing firms, and healthcare institutions.

Farmer is co-leader of McKinsey's global Business Building practice. This practice involves more than a quarter of the Firm leadership working on e-transformation, corporate growth and innovation, and new business creation around the world. Over the past year, McKinsey has been involved in helping clients launch over 350 new businesses. He served as office manager in Canada from 1991 to 1997. He is very involved in Firm governance and chaired the Firm committee responsible for electing new partners. In addition to serving on several other Firm management committees, he is a member of McKinsey's Shareholder Council which acts as McKinsey's board of directors.

Farmer received his BA and his MBA from the University of Western Ontario. Before joining McKinsey in 1978, he was a consultant with the Canadian federal government working on industrial development projects.

‘E-business got a lot of airtime, so much so that it's tempting to say that it was all talk and no substance, but I suspect the level of investment that's still going on is far higher than one might think. What's disappeared is all the e-nonsense: you now have corporations looking to use this technology in the business-to-employee context, in order to take out significant costs.

The same is true of the consulting industry. Of course, with the benefit of hindsight, it's easy to say that the reaction of the sector to e-business required just as much correction as the activity of the markets themselves. What we went through was an economic anomaly, and the pattern of demand since has fundamentally changed. Some pure e-consultancies are now trying to diversify, realising that they have a business model that simply doesn't go anywhere and hasn't proved capable of generating revenue per consultant of anything more than a fraction of that earned in the strategy segment of the consulting market – a problem that is now compounded by low rates of utilisation. And I think this demonstrates that public ownership makes a world of difference in this industry: it didn't take that much of a downturn among this group of firms for analysts and investors to declare the sector effectively dead.

That doesn't mean that these firms will have no lasting impact, if we look forward. They attracted a large number of very talented consultants, who were not only excellent in their chosen field of specialisation, but also very well-suited to a collaborative style of working. As a result, I think the pure e-consultancies may evolve in one of two directions: some – a minority – may become strategy boutiques; others may move more into the web-enabling part of the industry and this is probably where most of the predicted consolidation will take place. But these firms also had an impact at a conceptual level. They took a more creative approach to organisational design, and introduced new business models, which the industry is still in the process of evaluating and assimilating. Like the development of any new product, there's been an inevitably high failure rate, but that doesn't mean that nothing of value has been left as a result.

They also raised the amount of 'venturing' undertaken by consultants. This, in particular, has been very interesting, and I think we're at too early a stage to be able to judge the extent to which it has been a success or failure. It will be interesting to see how venture capital skills, combined with consulting, can be utilised to meet market expectations. Clearly, a privately-owned firm like McKinsey has a bias against that model, but I really don't see anything that's happened since mid-2000 that could convince me otherwise.

Another area in which the pure e-consultants have changed things is in the relationship between consulting firms and technology companies. What happens when a firm becomes a quasi-software house, focused on creating business solutions? Is the obvious strategy – of merging with a much larger technology company – the best way forward? Such unions might work in defined situations, where it's possible to codify knowledge and where the threat of a culture clash is minimal, but the reality is that most consulting firms don't lend themselves to this way of working. Especially where strategy consulting is concerned, every problem needs its own unique solution: there's no electronic bulletin board with the answer. At the same time, it's important to recognise that, for a consulting firm to work in this latter environment, and still manage to grow effectively, it needs structure and discipline: the more chaotically organised new firms certainly managed to grow rapidly in their early days, but many couldn't sustain this over time or when client demand changed.

And client demand has changed. For the last couple of years, the 'e' prefix has been used to legitimise very high fee rates. Chief executives, under pressure to respond, separated out the 'e' parts of their organisations – because this was an easy decision to make. While we are not wont to make specific predictions about the future, both of these factors will, I think, engender a resistance that will prevent clients from returning to the levels of expenditure seen in 1998–2000 in the foreseeable future. Now, they realise that their 'e' activities need to be integrated into their mainstream organisation, not isolated from it: similarly, e-consulting will be part of the whole, not a separate discipline. You only need to look at consulting expenditures in the wireless area to see this: the time-scales being adopted are much more reasonable; more rational assumptions are being made about penetration; crucially, rather than starting with business-to-consumer models, built around innovative technology, organisations recognise that the corporate market holds the promise of long-term profitability.

There's certainly increasing circumspection among clients. As a result we're already seeing some consolidation across the consulting industry. But that doesn't mean that mergers between firms will be the solution: on the evidence to date, there's nothing that suggests mergers will necessarily change the fundamental economics of the businesses involved. Some firms – particularly the niche players – may be acquired by others. But it could be argued that many firms may have to shrink in order to grow. A minority of the newer firms may well enter the strategy space, but I suspect this will be on a sector-specific basis: they'll become experts in the impact of technology on retail banks, for example.

Going forward, chief executives are looking for new sources of revenue growth – something that e-commerce has not yet delivered. Part of a role for firms like McKinsey will be to help companies think through and evaluate new business models. There's also a great opportunity in transforming businesses through the web and streamlining business processes for greater productivity. At the same time, clients are going to be far more focused on how they can make their organisations more effective – the next wave of knowledge management, if you like. Corporate portals, for instance, don't just provide an opportunity for the online delivery of business functions, but can change collective behaviour. We're already seeing a significant number of companies redirect their e-commerce activities to this end. As a result, I think we may also see a tendency for clients to look to consultants for more commodity solutions. This means there'll be pressure on strategy firms both to distance themselves from the commodity parts of the consulting industry – by providing even better insight – but also deliver this insight more efficiently.

Essentially, management faces three challenges: building, operating and trading businesses. The last of these has historically been the field of the investment bankers, and they're well-positioned for the lion's share of M&A work, but consultants have also made major contributions. 'Operate' is the market in which most consulting firms work, and it's a market that I think will become more crowded as software companies enter it. 'Build' is the market where clients may recognise McKinsey adding the greatest value: helping companies identify new ways to grow. And the single most important factor determining the success with which we can do this is – as it has always been – people. In fact, people become even more important during economic downturns, as we require extraordinary people if we're to justify the role we play with clients. Genuine talent continues to be a scarce commodity: you can't get a software package to design a new business model. The challenge for us is to ensure that we can attract the best people and the best clients: because we're privately owned, we can make long-term investments in both of these areas, without having to worry what the quarterly results will look like. We can focus on serving clients and developing people, not on short-term results. ’

25

Mercer Management Consulting

João Baptista and David Morrison

As one of the world's leading corporate strategy firms, Mercer Management Consulting helps leading enterprises achieve sustained shareholder value growth through the development and implementation of innovative business designs. Mercer's proprietary business design techniques, combined with its specialised industry knowledge and global reach, enable companies to anticipate changes in customer priorities and the competitive environment, and then design their businesses to seize opportunities created by those changes.

The firm's capabilities and leading-edge intellectual capital are enhanced by its industry expertise and geographic range. For 30 years, Mercer has worked with leaders of major companies in chemicals and pharmaceuticals, communications, computing, consumer goods, financial services, health care, media and entertainment, manufacturing, oil and gas, retail, transportation and utilities. The firm also offers special services in the areas of Internet strategy and private equity investing.

Mercer Management Consulting is part of Mercer Consulting Group, one of the world's largest consulting organisations. Together, the firms of Mercer Consulting Group have 14 000 employees in more than 30 countries throughout the world.

João Baptista, a Vice President in Mercer Management Consulting's London office, is worldwide head of Mercer's Communications, Information & Entertainment Group and a member of Mercer's Board of Directors. Baptista focuses on operator strategy and has led a variety of telecommunications projects, including strategic and operational turnarounds, investment and alliance strategies, business valuation and technology investment programmes. Most recently, he has assisted operators and media companies define and execute their IP and Internet-related initiatives. He has helped more than half the European telecommunications, CATV and media companies restructure various aspects of their operations in response to competitive and technology changes.

Baptista's other work at Mercer has encompassed a wide range of industries and specific assignments, including a buy-out evaluation in the consumer goods area, a turnaround strategy for an electrical equipment manufacturer, a specialty product strategy for downstream oil businesses and competitive strategies for both the paper industry and textile manufacturers. He has also authored numerous articles and conference papers on the telecommunications industry, and is co-author of the book *Grow to Be Great*, focusing on growth strategies.

Baptista received a degree in mechanical engineering from the Swiss Federal Institute of Technology in Lausanne, Switzerland and an MBA from the Stanford University School of Business.

' You have to separate the speculation and wishful thinking from the serious work which is still taking place in terms of web-enablement. There's no doubt the Internet provides a very cost-efficient means of automating processes. In this respect, you can see it as part of a continuum of technological development, but it's distinguished by the relative maturity of its public infrastructure, and this openness creates an opportunity for many processes to be automated than has hitherto been the case. Take a sales process for example: the catalogue can be online; the purchase transaction can take place online; customers can track their orders online. And the fact that these activities can now be performed at a fraction of their traditional cost means that web-based technologies are unquestionably here to stay. We're already seeing great improvements in productivity in the marketplace – companies managing to reduce their procurement costs by half, for example. Dell, despite the upheaval in the high-tech industry, is still able to undercut its competitors on price because its costs continue to be the lowest. Because they can keep their prices low, companies like Dell will be more resilient during an economic downturn: they can go where their competitors can't follow.

But in the middle of this period of genuine technological change, there was a surfeit of venture capital available. This meant that ideas in isolation, rather than business propositions (with customers, management capability and robust profit streams), got funded. Investors massed around a variety of new companies and ignored the fact that many established corporations were pursuing similar ideas, albeit more quietly, and from a far superior financial position.

Will any of this have a lasting impact on the consulting industry? I think it's more a question of a change of pace rather than a paradigm shift. I think many of the established consultancies will emerge stronger, with a greater awareness of managing a portfolio of clients, increased efficiency in the way in which they manage resources, and higher recruiting standards. Many of the new firms will have to restructure; others may become specialist boutiques. I don't believe these firms changed things radically: they certainly didn't revolutionise the industry, as some at the time claimed to be doing. Yes, they made much of the fact that they combined strategy and implementation, but, in reality, it's been twenty years since a consulting firm could be credible on the basis of its ideas alone: we've all recognised that actions speak louder than words.

The changes that have taken place have been driven by clients, not consulting firms. We're certainly seeing far more 'constellations' of clients coming together and sharing the outcome of consulting projects. The upside to this, from our perspective, is that if you do good work, your reputation grows very quickly. The best consultants have always taken measured risks and reacted very quickly to issues that arise, but these kinds of arrangements certainly raise the stakes in terms of the potential impact on a firm. The best consultants will also be prepared to invest money in projects in which they're involved. They become part of the constellation on a long-term basis, where their returns are tied into the success of the venture and where they're expected to be on their client's 'side'.

This is a trend we have perceived: clients expect us to partner with them. But does this mean that we'll be less likely to win work from their competitors in the future? Quite the reverse, we're finding. The fact we've worked for one company means that we've already built up a uniquely specialised knowledge base about that industry. In reality, it's often consultants who are being selective about the clients they work for. We want to work with companies that are prepared to involve us as an integral part of their own decision-making process. We don't want to work with people who are hiring us for a single transaction. The buoyant market of the last three to four years has allowed firms like ours to turn down work and give preference to those clients who want to involve us at the outset. It may be that the consulting market of the future is more polarised between those clients who are open to new ideas and those that want simply to replicate what someone else has already done, and Mercer Management Consulting is certainly trying to position itself in the former segment, to work with clients that are not afraid of radical restructuring if the occasion demands it.

It's perhaps harder for the very large consulting firms to do this, as differentiation is always more difficult. Will they break up? These are firms with extraordinary traditions, and they can deliver excellent work. Deciding to break any organisation up is a very hard decision for its management to take. It's almost always interpreted externally as an admission of failure – that a company has stalled – rather than an acknowledgement that it becomes increasingly difficult to extract value from an organisation as it grows bigger and more diverse. I think we're more likely to see these firms spinning off smaller businesses that have the focus and entrepreneurialism the parent lacks, but it's still going to take a lot of courage to do even this.

Do we need a different kind of consultant to thrive in this environment? Clients have to live and breathe their projects, and I think they've always wanted consultants who are prepared to do the same. This does mean that we have to pick consultants for their personality as well as their educational background. The counterpart of the kind of partnerships I've already mentioned is that clients tend to be much more open and often suggest how well consultants fit into the client's environment. The client might say to us 'X is a fantastic guy, but we don't think this role suits him…'

Looking to the future, I think there are two significant trends. First has been the level of investment in the global communications infrastructure – it's been similar to the investment made in the US interstate highway system in the 1950s, and it's not something that's going to go away. Second is the desire among consumers to be more mobile: no one wants to be fixed to one place anymore – you only have to look at the ubiquity of mobile phones to see that. But I don't see either of these trends adding up to the continuation of the excessive investment we have experienced during the last two years. I see more conventional levels of growth in the consulting industry, with companies returning to fundamental questions, such as how they create value for their customers. Consultants will continue to be catalysts, driving improvements in efficiency from sector to sector and client to client. ’

David Morrison is Vice-Chairman of Mercer Management Consulting and directs the firm's MercerDigital practice. In his 20 years of consulting, Morrison has worked with leading companies in the electronics, computer hardware and software, information services, e-commerce, Internet, healthcare, telecommunications and financial services industries.

Morrison is co-author, with Adrian Slywotzky, of *How Digital Is Your Business?*; *The Profit Zone: How Strategic Business Design Will*

Lead You to Tomorrow's Profits (a 1998 *Business Week* 'Top 10 Best' Business Book) and *Profit Patterns: 30 Ways to Anticipate and Profit from Strategic Forces Reshaping Your Business.* He has written articles for a number of important publications, including the 'Managers Journal' column of the *Wall Street Journal*, and also contributed to the development of the frameworks in Adrian Slywotzky's best-selling book *Value Migration.*

Morrison holds a BSAE from the US Naval Academy and served seven years in the US Navy as a Naval Flight Officer. He earned an MSE from Princeton, where he was awarded a Guggenheim Fellowship, and graduated with high distinction from the Harvard Business School, where he was named a Baker scholar.

‘In the late 1990s, companies were being valued at twenty times what they were worth and twenty times what we would pay for them. The hype was crazy, with everyone talking about 'amazoning' the old economy corporations. First it was business-to-consumer, then it was business-to-business: 900 to 1000 business-to-business exchanges had received funding by the middle of the year 2000, although most sectors could support one or two at best. What we're now experiencing feels a little bit like a bad hangover after a really big party: it's not just that things look so different in the cold light of day, but also that people feel embarrassed by their behaviour.

Personally, I like the shift. I see myself as what I jokingly call a 'business fundamentalist': when I talk to clients, I don't start off the conversation with 'look at what this amazing bit of technology could do for your business', but with 'let's think about how we can create value for this customer segment, and then think about the people, processes and tools you'll need in order to deliver that value'. And I think that's what went wrong over the last couple of years: people lost sight of the customer and what this new technology would actually do for them.

But I wouldn't say that nothing has changed as a result of e-business. Using Mercer as my 'sample', I think there'll be two significant differences going forward. First, it's clear that technology has become one of the vectors driving economic value. In the past, technology was more of an enabler – a means by which a business strategy could be achieved; today, it's clearly a critical factor which determines what you can and cannot do in strategic terms. Second, one of the messages that came out from the e-specialist firms was: 'Don't spend a lot of time developing your strategy. By the time you've finished planning, the market and your competitors will have moved on: much better to launch a trial and learn by the results.' It was strategy-on-a-flip-chart: you build a prototype, test it with your customers and iterate around the design until you have something that works. I don't believe that kind of approach made sense at the time, and it certainly doesn't now, when companies have realised that time to market shouldn't be used as an excuse to truncate their decision-making processes. That being said, clients still expect strategy assignments to be much shorter than they were ten years ago. You have to remember that in the days before spreadsheets, a large part of a strategy assignment was taken up in gathering and calibrating data, so it was neither uncommon nor unreasonable in the 1970s for an engagement to last between six and twelve months. Typically, clients today want the process to take no more than two to three months.

Putting these two factors together has, I believe, significant implications for the consulting industry. If you're working in an environment where your people are working on a continuous stream of high-pressure, comparatively short projects, with little opportunity for a break in between, then you're not only going to need a highly efficient resource allocation system, but also some means of building in recovery time if you're to prevent a high burn-out rate. When projects took longer, you'd expect peaks and troughs of pressure: you wouldn't be under the same intense pressure week in week out – and then be expected to start all over again as soon as one project had finished. Obviously, there are enormous implications for knowledge management: how can you make sure your people are doing the right thing – reapplying the proven intellectual capital the firm already has, rather than starting with a blank sheet of paper.

You also have to integrate your skills-base far more effectively. The process by which companies developed strategy used to be very logical and linear: you gathered data; assessed the situation; developed a set of strategic options; and analysed what human capital would be required to deliver the preferred option and what incentives had to be in place to motivate those involved. Finally, you'd identify what technology would be needed. In classic terms, operations followed strategy. But, today, strategy is more a function of the available human capital: your people determine what you can do. The same recognition is changing strategy consulting: it's not just a question of carrying out the analysis, but understanding the organisation well – what skills are available, and who'll be driving the strategy once it's agreed. This means we need consultants who can combine a highly analytical process with an awareness of human potential and constraints. Sometimes, particularly where we don't know a client well, this means we may need to bring in some specialist expertise in organisation analysis. However, where we've been working with a client over a long period of time, we generally find that we've acquired this knowledge, almost unconsciously, *via* the consulting process. That's what seems to work best from both our and our clients' perspectives – and I think it probably means we'll be concentrating on working with long-term clients even more than we have done in the past.

But there are clients who make this way of working very hard. You can go into a multinational and develop a strategy for, say, a specific product, only to find that one country isn't prepared to adopt it because of some local political issue. At this point the whole process of rolling-out the strategy can be disrupted: 95 per cent of the organisation is being held up by the remaining 5 per cent which doesn't agree. What you need – what the client needs – is a CEO who's prepared to stand up and build consensus. But sometimes what you get is a response that this is your problem as consultants. People seem to think that the analytical process of developing a strategy will in itself wave a magic wand to transform their organisation, that information in isolation is enough to get an organisation moving.

Will the need to become more involved in the human side of strategic execution change the client-consultant relationship in the future? I certainly think that outsourcing will continue to grow and cover more diverse parts of an organisation, but it seems to be that the main obstacle to consultants taking on an even wider role is economic. How would you pay them? When clients talk about sharing the upside and downside of a particular project, it tends to be the latter they're thinking about: once you turn this around and show them how much money they could end up paying you if you achieved the objectives set, then the vast majority balk at that kind of remuneration.

Of course, in the last couple of years, we have seen an increasing number of consulting firms taking equity stakes in their (smaller) clients' business. Some of these will work, I think, but perhaps as much through luck than design: some firms will simply have a winning ticket in the lottery; the vast majority won't. One of the main things will be to have a decent spread to your portfolio: if a typical venture capital firm might expect one in five of its investments to be a major win, a consulting firm that has limited its exposure by putting money in just two or three companies may well find that it loses on all of them. Succeeding in this field is also a matter of corporate culture. A good private equity firm has a very different culture to the 'let's all work together and see if we can solve this' culture of consultancy. Because the ability of venture capitalists to make future investments is a function of the internal rate of return of their current portfolio, they tend to be much tougher and less patient. Consultants, by contrast, tend to be more collaborative team players.

So what – if anything – will be the next focus of interest among clients? Whatever it is, it has to have real economic value attached to it. I think this is one of the key lessons from the last few years. Going back to the late 1980s, something like business process re-engineering, at least in its early manifestation, did have this, and that's one of the reasons why it was – in the relative terms of the consulting market – such a long-lived service line. But perhaps management enthusiasm is becoming a bit like the stock market, more volatile and increasingly driven by group dynamics than individual choice. One of the reasons for this is the changing relationship between consultancy and technology. When I started my consulting career in the 1970s, consultancy really meant strategy consultancy, and the industry was like a village in which everyone knew everyone else. What the big accounting firms were doing was technology implementation, not consultancy. But the stereotypical consultant today is in his or her late twenties, doing large systems installation at a client's site. Waves of demand for consultancy are therefore increasingly being driven by technology waves – the move from mainframes to client server technology in the early 1990s, package implementation in the mid-1990s, and, finally, Y2K. And with each wave, it becomes increasingly hard for a consulting firm to adapt: some are finding they can't – the partners leave the company name behind and go on to found new companies which don't have the legacy of their precursors. Today, we see this happening with the appearance of a new group of firms focusing solely on wireless applications, but you have to ask where the genuine value for customers is in that.

The mooted economic downturn will undoubtedly have an impact on this. Each previous downturn of recent years (1982–83 and 1990–91) has changed the consulting industry. Consulting remains a discretionary expense item, and you tend to see companies delaying projects to protect their earnings in a given quarter. This time around, I'd expect to see a big shake-out of people, reflecting the overcapacity of the industry even in today's market. But that doesn't mean that the 'war for talent' is over. As the pace of delivery accelerates, having the right people becomes even more important. Similarly, in an environment where a long-standing knowledge of a client's organisation determines both the quality of service and profitability, the retention of those people becomes essential. ’

26

The Sharma Group

Panna Sharma

Panna Sharma was Chief Strategy Officer at Atlanta-based iXL, where he was responsible for articulating iXL's global strategy, identifying growth opportunities in new geographic, vertical and horizontal markets and driving the evolution of iXL's delivery methodology. As resident visionary on iXL's leadership team, Panna led the company's global effort to reinvent professional services for a network economy.

'The e-business market matured far more quickly than anyone expected, driven by a combination of the first signs of a global economic downturn with a sudden switch on the part of investors from optimism to pessimism. As a result, 'e-business' has become part of what we think of as 'business'. But does that translate into going back to 'business as usual' in the consulting industry? I don't think so.

I see three major changes occurring within the industry, all of which have significant implications for the future. First, there's the way in which clients buy consultancy. More and more, they're looking to combine their purchase of consultancy with their hardware and software purchase decisions. They want to buy blue-chip technology with turnkey consulting skills to help implement it: they want competent programme managers who are capable of bridging the gap between the strategic objectives of the investment and the practical issues involved in delivery. It was this integration of strategy and technology which distinguished e-consulting firms in the late 1990s and which has created a benchmark in clients' expectations since then. It wasn't just that a more integrated approach offered clients a better quality of service, but simple economics: savvy IT managers began to ask why they should be pay the premium fee-rates of traditional consulting firms, when they could get an equivalent level of service from the technology provider, but – bundled in with the cost of the technology itself – at a much lower price.

This trend in buying behaviour ought to have acted in favour of these new consulting firms, but another factor has worked against them. Since mid-2000, I've seen a healthy and welcome migration among clients back to proving a business case. As everyone now recognises, expenditure on e-business ideas had become over-zealous; there was too much emphasis on being first to market and developing strategies within a 90, 60 or even 30 day period. That kind of behaviour has now ceased: clients are much less willing to accept what a consulting firm is telling them at face value, and – typically – they've returned to taking between four and six months to evaluate and approve a business case. Many of them found themselves running multiple projects, based on poorly thought-out ideas, and which now required considerable work just to wind them down. Not surprisingly, clients have started to force consulting companies to invest more heavily in checking through the business cases they help develop, often for free, before the start of the engagement proper. The development of the business case has, in effect, become part of the sales process and this has, I think, injected a healthy dose of entrepreneurialism into the consulting industry. But the e-consulting firms found it hard to cope with this shift: they lost out, not because the revenue wasn't there, but because they lacked both the client relationship and sales processes necessary to sustain a long sales cycle, and patience on the part of their investors.

For e-consulting firms, survival will be solely determined by available cash. The public ownership structures of these firms has been a problem, not because any financial problems are far more visible than they would be with a privately-held partnership, but because they are forced to take account of the views of shareholders who aren't close to the consultancy and who have little insight into what the firm should do, in the short and long term, to secure its future. Consulting isn't like making cans of beans: when times are tough, a consulting firm can't decide to close up shop for a few months; you can't keep a warehouse of consultants, ready to come out when the upturn comes. In fact, I think all the e-consulting firms which are publicly-held will be forced to move into other non-consulting activities in order to survive.

The established strategy consultancies are clearly better able to withstand these changes, but – in most cases – technology remains their Achilles heel. It's very clear that, at the moment, clients are looking for specific ideas to create new value in a new market, with a new product or *via* a more efficient process. Technology is a critical component of this – one of the key value drivers – and I'd argue that a consulting firm not in a position to discuss it will rapidly lose credibility in the future. The larger strategy firms will also find themselves under threat from investment banks.

We've already seen, during the California fuel crisis, for instance, investment banks (in this case, Goldman Sachs) being invited in to help identify a way out of the crisis – a role that consultants have traditionally played. Of course, consulting firms have also tried to move into the investment banking industry, but they remain at a disadvantage: investment banks have a financial structure capable of underwriting their consultancy work, but consulting firms aren't typically equipped to underwrite their banking work.

However, I think it's the larger firms who are most at risk from the entry of investment banks into the consulting market space. One of the trends I certainly see continuing in the future is the increased 'atomisation' of the industry. Already clients are much less willing to hire consultants to carry out an overall rethink of their strategy, and are much more likely to hire them for a precise need – to develop, for instance, a strategy for a specific customer segment in a given geographical market. Niche strategy firms, in particular, will be the beneficiaries of this shift, and there's already evidence of larger firms making 'pin-point' mergers with such firms to ensure their coverage. It's also a trend which inevitably raises questions about the viability of firms that try to be all things to all people.

Offshore development companies (ODCs) – like those based in the Far East that undertake some aspects of delivery at far lower prices than those charged by equivalent companies based in developed economies – are complicating this picture further. With major clients now outsourcing significant projects to such companies, there's no question but that labour arbitrage will become a significant factor in the consulting market. Being able to take advantage of the cost differentials by securing deals with ODCs will become a matter of economic survival.

Another thing that's clear from the last couple of years is that the kind of corporate venturing undertaken by many consulting firms isn't working. With so many investments faring so badly, it's going to be some time before we see the consulting industry making significant forays in this direction again. It's not that the theory's faulty – consulting companies should be a source of new ideas and the whole rationale of venturing is to take new ideas and realise them, so there's an immediate synergy there – it's just that no one has yet cracked the code of doing this kind of work on a profitable basis. Instead, what I'm sure we'll see is a whole wave of acquisitions, as the larger consulting firms and technology companies seize the opportunity of the low valuations of e-consulting firms. The survivors are so cheap that few of the big firms are going to be able to resist the temptation: the era of the pure e-consultancy is over.

So what's the next big thing? Despite the threatened economic downturn,

I'm optimistic about the global economy, and the role of consultants in it. There are enormous opportunities opening up to do business in the Middle East, India and China. The commercialisation of these economies alone is likely to generate an unprecedented amount of consultancy. Technology – the development of the next generation of networks – will also continue to be a major driver of change, and therefore consultancy. Another important trend I foresee is more business-to-business supplier networks being formed, which look to reinvent the value chain for their industry, be that microchips, plastics or whatever. This activity will create a considerable incremental demand for consultancy, but for the group of companies as a whole, rather than for any one of them in isolation. Thus, for example, a company and its suppliers will jointly hire a firm to develop a common strategy across their shared value chain. Such developments represent a challenge as much as an opportunity for the consulting industry, as working with multiple clients will stretch the client relationship management processes of most firms. Historically, consulting firms have tended to rely on smart individuals to win and deliver business, and one of the lessons of the last two years has been the need to institutionalise these skills, by managing client service on a far more proactive basis. Working with multiple clients simultaneously – many of whom may have subsidiary agendas – will mean that consulting firms have to reinvent their approach to client service. But for firms that can do that, and can remain very clearly focused on where they add value, future prospects look excellent. ’

27

Razorfish

Michael Moore

Razorfish is a global digital solutions provider that consults with companies on business and brand strategy, design and technology, partnering with its clients to increase revenues, reduce costs and enhance productivity to maximize competitive advantage. Its aim is to strengthen an organization's relationships with its key constituents *via* the creation of superior user experiences, and its work spans a breadth of platforms, devices and networks – from integration with legacy systems, development of business applications and device-based functionality delivered *via* broadband, broadcast, web and wireless.

Razorfish employs more than one thousand professionals worldwide, with headquarters in New York and offices in Amsterdam, Boston, Frankfurt, Hamburg, Helsinki, Los Angeles, London, Milan, Munich, New York, Oslo, San Francisco, San Jose, Stockholm, and Tokyo. Razorfish has worked with hundreds of leading organizations around the world, including clients such as Ford, DuPont, Nissan-Europe, Disney, Time Warner, Viacom, Deutsche Bank, Fidelity Investments and Charles Schwab.

Michael Moore has been the managing director of Razorfish Amsterdam since the offices opened in July 1998. He was responsible for Razorfish's Benelux activities which have flourished under his leadership. Moore has witnessed great change in a short period of time as the office has moved from Conduit Communications to I-Cube and then to Razorfish. Despite this, Amsterdam operations have continued to develop at a rapid pace. Along with the numerous clients relationships that he was involved in, he was also proud to look after an ever growing team of digital strategists, designers and technologists at the office in Amsterdam.

Since October 2000, Moore has been the Executive Vice-President Europe, where his aim is to ensure that Europe plays its part in contributing to Razorfish's goal of becoming the leading end-to end digital solutions partner on this continent.

‘The impact of 2000 has been to make it abundantly clear how important it is for consulting firms to productise their service offering. It used to be that consultants could win business just by saying that they were smart. Today, they need something specific to talk about: they want something tangible, not an esoteric theory. You can’t get away with saying you’ve got a bunch of bright people – intellectual capital needs to be backed up by technology.

That’s a real challenge for the pure strategy consultancies who could justify their positioning back in the days when technology meant coding, but are now faced with an environment in which technology can have an enormous impact on a business at a strategic level. They may be well-equipped to help with a conventional value adding strategy – a new acquisition, or increased penetration of a given market segment, for instance – but it’s difficult to see how they can continue to be credible with clients if they can’t talk about the potential value-add from technology.

But the implications for the consulting industry don’t stop with the strategy firms. One of the most important changes wrought by e-business has been to demonstrate that strategy and technology are now forever interlinked. Everyone has to come up with a solution: everyone has to do something. This isn’t a paradigm shift: the seeds of this have been apparent for years – if we look back over the last fifty years or so, it’s clear that the rate at which technological changes have to be assimilated into business strategy is increasing exponentially. It’s now reached a point where no consulting firm can ignore it.

Moreover, as any market develops, the businesses within it will tend to shift from trying to be all things to all people to focusing on specific niches where they perceive themselves to have a competitive advantage. This is certainly true of the consulting industry: there’s no one at the moment who’s claiming to provide a genuine end-to-end service: everyone’s picking their particular space. That makes things easier from the buyer’s perspective, and I think it suggests, first, that the one-stop-shopping model of consultancy isn’t going to be viable in the long term and, second, that the consulting firms which pursue the one-stop-shop strategy will end up never doing leading-edge work in any area because clients don’t see them as being sufficiently specialised. The last couple of years have also been an object lesson in brand building within the consulting industry. The fact that companies, like Razorfish, were able to come along and establish a strong brand image in just a handful of years, is testimony to the importance of having a focused service offering. It’s raised the stakes in terms of what is possible over a given period, and I’m in no doubt that we’ll see a massive increase in expenditure on branding by the more established firms over the next few years. We've already seen a shift, away from firms promoting themselves *via* their clients' success, to an environment in which firms issue press releases immediately on the acquisition of a new client or contract.

Which of the new generation of consulting firms will survive? Financial strength – or at least the appearance of it – is most obvious factor that will determine success in the future. Firms like Razorfish are suffering at the moment because the restructuring the company is going through is so visible: a private partnership going through similar pain – as I suspect many of them are – can conceal this from clients and the press. But looking beyond this, I think survival is going to depend on the extent to which they've managed to create an integrated organisation. Too many firms, rolling up countless acquisitions, became groups of dots on a map, but genuine integration goes far beyond this and includes having a strong, common culture and delivery methodology. The survivors will have this, and will be honest and open with clients about what they can and cannot do. It goes back to the point I made earlier about the need for focus and specialisation: if a firm like Razorfish is clear about what it does – digital and technical strategies – then we can live side by side with the more established firms that focus on, say, software implementation and delivery. In fact, we believe partnerships will be an important source of growth within the consulting industry in the future: there are already examples of consulting firms that have partnered with technology companies and seen their growth rates quadruple as a result of the flow of sales opportunities coming through from the technology side.

But there are limits to partnering. One important lesson I think the industry has learned is that consulting firms don't necessarily make good venture capitalists. A lot of firms used the stock market booms of 1998–2000 to justify taking equity stakes in clients in return for services. In all but a handful of cases, this strategy is dead. Where it has worked, it's been because it's on a comparatively small scale – more like the partners of the firms choosing to invest in a small number of specific opportunities – rather than the firm trying to provide capital on a more systematic, institutionalised basis. At the time, people said that it was the logical extension of the type of payment-by-results arrangements that appeared during the 1990s, but I actually think that even that was over-stated. A friend once said to me that he'd tell clients he was prepared to do this, primarily as a means of distancing himself from the competition (who weren't); however, once the detailed discussions took place, the client would invariably find that, although it was quite easy to measure the downside to a project, finding a way to quantify the upside was difficult, if not impossible.

The real sea-change we saw in client behaviour happened in the middle of 2000: almost overnight, people seemed to be much clearer about what they wanted and how much they were prepared to pay for it. This was matched by a shift back towards the IT department being the main purchaser of consultancy: prior to this, we'd found ourselves talking to people in all parts of a client's organisation. Clients want to be clearer about the value that consultants add. In the mid-1990s, a typical client would be looking to analyse the return on investment of a given consulting engagement at its conclusion; what we're seeing today is clients asking for this kind of analysis up-front, as part of the sales process.

But as one consulting market matures, another one will emerge. However big an individual's ego, there's always some point on which he or she is uncertain, and where uncertainty exists, there'll always be a need for some sort of objective, independent advice. And the fundamentals of giving that advice, delivering results and building client relationships don't change.

But there always will be a 'next big thing', and it's amazing how short people's memories tend to be. Once people start to recognise the kinds of applications they will be able to run over fixed and mobile broadband communications, I suspect we'll see another wave of collective enthusiasm – perhaps less marked and more gradual than the burst of activity we've seen over the last two to three years, but significant nonetheless. At the moment, business still sees this technology as just a means of creating more sophisticated web-sites, but the potential is much larger than that. But the fact that clients will still need consultants doesn't mean that consulting firms can afford to be complacent about the future. There's a storm brewing in the industry, with even the largest, most established players talking about downsizing and laying off staff: people at all levels of experience – from the least to the most highly-skilled – are coming on the market at once. The need for consultancy may be never-ending, but for many individual consultants and, I suspect, many firms, the industry is going to seem a lot less attractive in the immediate future than it has appeared to be in the past. ’

28

Scient

Charlie Blackburn

Scient is an e-business consultancy which uses its extensive e-business experience and expertise to reduce cost and create revenue opportunities. Since its founding in 1998, Scient's only business has been e-business, from strategy development through to implementation. The differentated approach which clients come to Scient for is a blend of strategy, customer experience (branding, fulfilment and usability) and technology.

Charlie Blackburn is Vice-President of Europe for Scient, based out of London. His focus is on e-business development and the transformation of traditional organisations through innovation. He has consulted for Scient's clients in the financial services and enterprise business units, developing and implementing e-business strategies. Blackburn was previously with a California-based consulting start-up, Pyramid Consulting, running its capital markets practice and founding their New York office. Before this, he was also employed by Accenture for eight years focusing on ERP and MRP solutions in a variety of industrial organisations.

‘It's my view that technology is continuing – and will continue – to create significant top and bottom-line opportunities for clients – and therefore for the consulting industry. We're seeing a lot of good business propositions being picked up by blue-chip corporations in order to transform their existing products and services, and even to create new ones. And, for all the media coverage of dot.com failures, there are still going to be a very large number of companies who are grappling with the question of how best to integrate ‘old’ and ‘new’ economy businesses. What kind of architecture do I need that can handle the complexity of a new venture while also linking it to my organisation's legacy systems? How do I rationalise my infrastructure?

But one of the issues we – as consultants – have to manage is technology's perennial ability to disappoint, which means that the investment dries up. There's undoubtedly a growing sense of technology 'fatigue' – or at least fatigue about the hype of technology, driven partly by the changing fortunes of technology companies but also by Y2K – the end of the world that didn't happen. Does that mean that we're more likely to have a fragmented technology market, as clients resist the pressure to create the kind of monolithic companies that dominated the industry prior to e-business? I think that would actually be to misunderstand the nature of the technology itself. Contrary to popular mythology, web-based strategies often have to be far more centralised than the strategies they replaced. You have to bring together disparate sources of data and ensure people can have access to them. In many cases, you see IT directors having to wrest control back from business units because the decisions about which platforms to use have to be made for the organisation as a whole. Furthermore, clients have already learnt that, if you want specialist technology resources, you have to go to a hardware or software developer, not to a more generically skilled consulting intermediary. This trend will, in turn, tend to consolidate demand around the sub-set of suppliers able to provide implementation services. Finally, you also have to think about the maintenance implications: it makes economic sense to consolidate around a small number of vendors once a technology has reached a particular level of maturity. New technologies will constantly emerge that fragment the market, and make technology purchase decisions more complex, but companies will try to offset this problem by limiting their options in other areas.

To differentiate themselves from both the large scale technology companies and the more generic consultancies, I believe that successful consulting firms will have to integrate in-depth technology skills with strategic and creative capabilities. A lot of firms haven't recognised this yet, and they certainly have no idea how difficult it is in practice. It means going beyond thinking about your immediate client to being able to understand the view of your client's customers. Take a question like the vision for your brand in a multi-channel environment: you can't answer that question if you've access to just strategy skills, or just technology skills, or just creative skills. Coming up with the right answer will require all three perspectives. You've also got to go and talk to the end-consumers, and these might be people your client rarely meets – as is the case with investment banks, who may see their clients very irregularly. To allow you to do this, your client has to trust you. The majority of traditional consulting firms still focus on keeping their immediate client – the internal executives – happy, but as soon as you start to judge your success on the basis of your client's success, you have to go beyond this and look at your client's end markets.

Another factor here is that consulting projects will become far more visible. One of the problems with business process re-engineering was that the process of implementation was complex – value wasn't generated where people expected it. By contrast, consulting projects today already have a much higher degree of transparency: we put much more effort into, for example, developing prototypes and testing them with customers, rather than writing detailed functional specifications. 'Don't give me all this paperwork', is what clients are saying. 'Give me something I can show to people and get feedback.' Again, this is driving the integration of strategic, technology and creative skills: if your starting point is a prototype system, not a document, then you have to look at issues like usability from the outset, and as an integral part of the process, not as a subsidiary part of it.

As far as Scient is concerned, we don't see anything over last few years – or in the next few – that will change our most important challenge, which is building the integration of these three crucial skills into the fabric of our organisation. I suppose it's inevitable that the incumbent players will try to write us – and other firms founded at the same time – out of history. But we have had an impact, not least because we managed to put this issue – the integration of different skill sets – to the top of many firms' internal agendas. It doesn't really matter that the industry may put people back in suits (and put them back into casual clothes a couple of years later): what matters is its ability to step outside the quite rigid division of skills which continues to be true of most incumbent consulting firms today. Integration – genuine integration – is something you really have to work at: you have to think about how you can rotate people, so they don't become stale, while also maintaining and developing their specialist know-how.

I suspect that many firms will chose the comparatively easy option of partnering with other firms – something that actually strengthens, rather than blurs, the boundaries between skills. I don't think we'll see this strategy producing many high performing teams. Another approach being tried is to create spin-out companies which can distance themselves from the culture of the parent firm and enable consultants to work in more dynamic, flexible ways. But this strategy is being limited by, on the one hand, the fact that these offshoots tend to be focused on certain types of project and, on the other, by the extent to which they continue to be dependent on the infrastructure of the parent. At Scient, we believe that our culture is one that does allow each of these skills to be treated equally, but we're continually looking for better ways of achieving integration.

We have to be clear about what we do well and what we can't do, as clients will become increasingly precise about what they want from their consultants. This doesn't mean, in my view, that the client-consultant relationship will become simply a series of discrete projects; rather, I think that firms will have long-term relationships but this will take the form of a continuous dialogue about the client's needs and our capabilities, instead of non-stop work. We're already seeing a return to the more exhaustive buying process that characterised the market in the early to mid 1990s, although this time clients want to capture some of the softer issues which subsequently came to the fore – our values and culture, for example. And the fact that buyers currently hold the balance of power in the relationship is one of the reasons why the client-consultant relationship, while being more effectively aligned around a shared set of objectives, will not disappear entirely. That's one reason why Scient largely involved the temptation of taking 'sweat equity' in client ventures. To be honest, we also thought we wouldn't be that good at playing the role of the venture capitalist, and we therefore limited our involvement to taking comparatively small stakes in second and third round funding. We're consultants for a reason – because we don't want to be entrepreneurs or venture capitalists.

And I think the opportunities for consultants in the future will be substantial – even if the market is difficult in the immediate term. The technology now becoming available will provide a major impetus to companies looking to outsource their non-core business activities. That in turn will mean that the outsourcing companies will be able to lock up the overwhelming majority of a corporation's expenditure in these areas: in effect, the corporation's IT budget will be being spent by the outsourcing company, not the people we currently regard as the client. Much of this expenditure, I'd argue, will go on commodity work: there are companies appearing that will, for example, take over an organisation's HR systems and provide a managed service. At the other extreme – and this is the market in which we see Scient continuing to work – new, emerging technologies will always disrupt the business continuum. 'E-business' was essentially about the Internet's power to collect and disseminate information, and information has, in effect, turbo-charged the impact of technology. Corporations can now consider radical strategies for outsourcing the vast majority of their non-core business activities and optimise their organisations around their best capabilities. They'll tend to retain the front-end parts of their business under their own control – their brand, their customer interfaces, and so on. But, in the back office, the shift towards managed services is going to have a significant impact in almost every sector – we'll have an economy in which almost everyone else is digitally connected to everyone else. 'Best practice' won't always win – we know that already, from the adoption of the VHS video-tape standard onwards: what will determine success will be which eco-system you belong to, who your partners are. I think we'll see consulting firms mirroring this structure: outsourcing, managed services, systems integration will all provide a massive source of business, but some of this work will be on a more commodity basis, some will be for consortia of clients, rather than individual ones. At the other – the front – end of the market, there'll be firms like Scient that focus on the impact of emerging technology on the customer interface. The issue for firms like ours will be maintaining the right degree of focus. Become too broad and we'll be in danger of looking like a generalist consultancy in the client's eyes; become too narrow and we won't be able to offer the range of opportunity that will attract the right people. ’

29

The Parthenon Group

Anthony Tjan

The Parthenon Group is a boutique strategy consulting firm with offices in Boston, San Francisco and London. The firm has a long history of serving senior executives and CEOs throughout the world on a wide range of issues including corporate and business unit strategy, merger and post-merger strategy, and innovation and strategic growth planning. The Parthenon Group has perhaps best been known for its deep and long-term relationships with a leading group of Fortune 1000 clients and was also pioneering in its fee-for-equity business model in its work with select high growth firms.

Anthony Tjan is a recognised business and technology thought-leader, successful entrepreneur, and a senior adviser to several top CEO's. Tjan is the Advisory Vice-Chairman and Senior Partner at Parthenon, a boutique strategy consulting firm with offices in Boston, San Francisco and London. He is also a Belfer Center and CGB (Center for Government and Business) Fellow at the Harvard Kennedy School of Government. Prior to Parthenon and his appointment at Harvard, Tjan served as Director and Executive Vice-President of ZEFER, an Internet-focused strategy consulting firm that he founded in 1998 with former colleagues from McKinsey & Company and Harvard Business School. At ZEFER, Tjan was one of the key driving forces in helping the company shape its vision and achieve rapid growth to more than 500 professionals in less than three years.

Today, Tjan continues to serve as a senior advisor to Fortune 500 CEOs and governments throughout the world; he is also Entrepreneur in Residence and Executive Director of Mosaic Venture Partner's Digital Media practice.

Tjan is a frequent commentator for, and has been regularly profiled in, national and international press including Wall Street Journal, Business Week, Financial Times, MSNBC, CNBC, and CNN. He has contributed as a columnist and authored more than 20 articles for leading business and technology publications including the Red Herring, Punto.Com, and Harvard Business Review. In addition, he sits on the boards or advisory boards of Screaming Media, Punto.com, Monitor & Company's On the Frontier, and OpenCOLA. Tjan holds an AB degree from Harvard College and an MBA from Harvard Business School.

'There's no question in my mind not only that the recent rise, fall, and stabilisation of 'new-age e-consultancies' did change the consulting industry over the last couple of years, but that many of those changes will be lasting. I come to this conclusion from having had the opportunity to be the founder of an Internet-focused consulting firm and reflecting back on that experience with my past work at McKinsey & Company and my current association with a leading strategy boutique firm, The Parthenon Group.

In the first place, the e-consulting firms have shed light on the importance of being genuinely multi-disciplinary. Particularly in the areas of e-business strategy, innovation, and growth strategy, they have shown that the consulting firm of the future needs more than MBA graduates: it needs, for example, people who understand that novel ideas and insights will be driven primarily by technology and designing new customer experiences. This means having professionals who understand intechnology and who can exploit it in the context of what people like James Gilmore have described as an 'experience-based economy'. Second, and by extension, these firms have reinforced – re-energised even – the need for a consulting firm to build its capabilities around innovative thinking. Whatever you think about the aberrations of Internet ventures and their market valuations since the late 1990s, you cannot argue about the impact of the Internet on large business cultures globally. Going forward, the successful ones will be those that can manage the kind of innovative thinking we have seen in the last two to three years, but with the right set of strategic filters and implemented at a more realistic pace that allows for better integration with existing capabilities. Indeed, the commercialisation of the Internet has reminded us once again of our tendency to overestimate short-term impact and underestimate the long-term effects.

I think you can also say that the e-consultancies have had quite profound effect on the culture of consulting firms themselves, essentially by changing the balance of reasons why an individual joins a consulting firm. Perhaps what I have learned most in founding the Internet consultancy, ZEFER, has been that a truly distinctive employee culture can wield tremendous firm value in the form of not only greater retention, but also unparalleled commitment and focus on continued improvement. This next generation consulting culture needs to be as focused as much on the employee value proposition as the client value proposition – in fact it can be argued that a significant part of client value is derived from having the right employee value proposition. Traditionally, people have entered the field of consultancy primarily because they want to learn new business and client management skills. To this, the newer consulting firms have stressed other cultural elements, such as a more diverse and open culture that rewards learning, offers greater risk-taking opportunities, and provides significantly greater degrees of diverse collaboration. Many of the newer e-consultancies have placed business, design, and technology professionals sitting side-by-side in an open office environment with no visible hierarchical divides. I get letters and emails all the time from people who fear that the recent economic volatilities may not allow for the continuation of an open and employee-centric culture as companies go back to things with which they are comfortable. What they are saying is not how they might miss the extrinsic fringe perks such as free beer and soda, and companion travel, but rather the more intrinsic cultural elements of open collaboration, freedom for significant risk-taking, and meritocratic career growth based not on age or credentials but simply value-delivered. There's a whole generation of young consultants whose formative experience have been in one of the 'new economy cultures', and that has implications for all the organisations they go on to work for.

The e-consulting firms also offered not only a learning environment, but challenged the very partnership ownership structure prevalent in established firms. Indeed over the last three years, established players recognised the importance of ownership or profit-sharing – below the partnership level - as a critical vehicle for attraction and retention. Almost all consulting firms found ways to adjust their compensation and today, for the most part, there is a balanced approach that is emerging in new and traditional consulting firms.

Going forward, it's clear that a firm's staying power depends heavily on its ability to combine effective professional development and learning at the individual level (the advantage of the more established firms) with the cultural openness, pro risk-taking and different 'look and feel' of the newer firms. The conventional, lock-step career path of the consultant will be challenged, as firms recognise that their organisation is a collection of diverse individuals who develop differently and at different paces, but who are still capable of making an enormous contribution to the firm. The days of the homogeneous career structure are over.

Less, perhaps, has changed on the client side. We may have gone through a period in which almost anyone could sell almost anything to almost anyone, but it's turned full-circle: clients are returning to the fundamental reasons for buying consultancy – the need for objective advice, the ability to help an organisation expand its capabilities and set the appropriate strategic growth agenda, and prioritise value-generating activities. Where there has been a change, it's been in clients' expectations. The world is now less about the need for speed and more about being first to finish the race, rather than being the first one out of the blocks. Clients have also realized that the value of a firm is more in the specific team and partner relationships than with the consulting institution itself. Boutique consulting firms, such as Parthenon, are particularly well positioned to maintain their strength in having fewer, but deeper and lasting client relationships. The hyper-growth of e-consulting firms and the already large size of the traditional consulting incumbents have made it more difficult to ensure consistency in quality of work.

In addition to having to do things ever more quickly, future consulting firms will have to find tangible ways to measure the value they deliver. The only way that consulting firms can continue to justify high fee rates and ensure stable revenue during economic downturns is by turning ideas into real implementation. To ensure that consultants have an alignment with the client objectives and results may mean more innovative ways of structuring client/consultant relationships. It may mean, for example, increasingly taking equity stakes in clients' ventures – as this is one of the most effective means of aligning interests. Too many firms during the dot.com boom tried to jump on the client-equity bandwagon for the wrong reasons. Euphoric markets encouraged short-term value-capture motivations, as opposed to a focus on long-term value creation. In many cases this led to poor client selection. The ability to use fee-for-equity takes significant experience and a principal investment mindset that takes years to develop. Parthenon, for example, has used this model with great success, but it has been a part of the company for over ten years, and it has required things such as a long-term client commitment, principal investment and due diligence expertise, and strong operational capabilities.

Consulting firms wishing to take selective advantage of the fee-for-equity model will have to look for and judge companies that have great potential value but which may be at a very early stage of development. Such arrangements therefore will probably only be appropriate to a subset of a client base, and more appropriate probably for regionally based-consulting firms with a relatively small partnership group, rather than large global consulting firms, where the risk/reward profile is difficult to justify on a large base of revenues. As a result, only a few consulting firms will operate with fee-for-equity. However – managed effectively – I'm in no doubt that this strategy will offer much higher levels of revenue per consultant than conventional consulting, once you take into account not only the time and materials billing but also the extraordinary gains from investments.

For several of the recently-born and smaller consulting firms, the next few years will probably be a period of consolidation, as we see who the real survivors and winners are going to be. The traditional strategy consultancies will benefit from a continuing drive for innovation, their depth of intellectual capital, and the sheer scale they have with a large number of employees. Specialty and boutique strategy-consulting firms will need to continue to find ways to differentiate themselves that go beyond regional relationships – they will have to pick key areas of intellectual capital to pursue and look towards innovative ways to gain greater leverage in their business model. The multitude of IT-focused consulting firms that exist at the moment will consolidate around two or three leading players with some highly specialized boutique players in areas such as security, content management, or supply chain integration.

And what will be the next 'big thing' that these firms will be doing? In my mind, it will centre around innovation and growth strategies which are already top issues for today's CEO and further popularised by business authors such as Clayton Christensen. While cost-reduction studies, post-merger integration, and organisational redesign will remain an important part of the mainstay of consulting, few firms have effectively deciphered the code on how to institutionalise innovation – for themselves and for their clients. Advising senior executives on innovation will require a different profile than the typical management consultant. Why? First, innovation requires an ability to have a view out to the future, or at minimum being able to explain the most relevant future trends in areas such as technology and design. This goes back to the earlier point, that the adviser of innovation will be an individual who is multidisciplinary and who can help express the future customer experience. Some of the industries that will be changed by technology and require significant innovation will first be those that are primarily made up of digital assets or digitisable assets – this includes media and entertainment, financial, publishing, and other knowledge-based sectors. How will we consume content in the future and on what platforms? How will pervasive technologies impact the way we conduct financial transactions? Other industries will be reshaped by the desire for new customer experiences – beyond the industries mentioned, they include transportation, several retail and consumer packaged goods firms. Will the automotive industry eventually make more money in the communications business than in financing or selling cars? What is the next winning retail concept that truly creates a new customer experience and is able to monetise it?

Answering these questions – and, even more importantly, being able to acquire the knowledge to answer such questions in the future – will involve consultants in at least four ways. They'll assist first with option generation; they'll help with the process of categorising and prioritising the options; they'll take the preferred option and prototype it; and they'll take the prototyped option and build it up into a sustainable business. Most traditional consultancies will focus on identifying and prioritising opportunities based on proven fact-based approaches: the challenge for them will be new idea generation and implementation. Indeed the first of these consultant opportunities to help generate and communicate new business concepts is by far the most intriguing. And not all consultancies will have the capabilities to do this. This is where the innovative thinking and potentially greatest value creation within the consulting market will take place in the future. ’

Index